A VERY PERSONAL FINANCE STORY

REFLECTIONS ON FAMILY, LOVE AND MONEY

CHRIS GARDNER

Christopher H. Gardner
FMF&E Wealth Management, LLC
5010 Campuswood Drive
East Syracuse, NY 13057

Printed in the United States of America.

To Lori, Austin, Charlotte, Areya, Nathan and Charlie.
You make me grateful every day.

Contents

WHY I WROTE THIS BOOK

I wrote this book to help anyone who has a hard time wrapping their head around their financial future. For anyone who feels the financial services industry has dragged personal finance down a rabbit hole of products, lingo, false hopes and confusing numbers. For anyone who hopes to find peace of mind about his or her finances.

A good personal financial plan can't be just about numbers. It also has to be about your hopes, dreams, fears and goals. It has to focus on what matters most to you, and it needs to be in a language you understand.

I have written this book with no charts and graphs, few numbers and, I hope, very little jargon. It includes a collection of my life experiences because these experiences have so strongly shaped my belief system. These experiences have taught me that life and financial issues are tightly interwoven and that life issues are usually far more important.

I have had several life experiences that have moved me along my path, but all of these pale in comparison to what happened in April 2016 with the birth of my identical twin boys, Nathan and Charlie.

Nathan and Charlie were born 15 weeks premature. As excited as I was, their grim medical condition turned my world on its head. Their extended stay in the Neonatal Intensive Care Unit changed the way I look at everything, especially health, faith and family.

We are all collections of life experiences, hopes and dreams. Against this backdrop, most of us are simply looking for a little balance in, and control over, our money and financial issues. I hope this book helps you look at your finances in new ways and offers useful ideas in pursuing your financial goals – the selection of an advisor, the investment of your money, and the way you think about and talk about your money.

To help you on that path, every chapter ends with a question or two to discuss with your advisor, and the last chapter offers ideas on how to find an advisor that's right for you.

INTRODUCTION

A few months ago, we celebrated our identical twin sons' first birthdays. It was an amazing day. A day that, at times, didn't seem possible.

Nathan and Charlie are truly miracle babies.

The twins were simply born too early. My wife, Lori, was only 25 weeks pregnant when she gave birth. That's more than three months short of a full-term pregnancy. The twins were so early, we hadn't even picked out names. For the first few days, they were simply "Baby A" and "Baby B."

It's hard to explain what a 25-week-old baby looks like. They each weighed less than two pounds. Their skin was so translucent you could see the outline of their internal organs. Their ears were still fully attached to their heads, with no flaps. They looked like a combination of an alien and a baby bird.

Nothing had prepared me for this. They were so tiny compared to Austin and Charlotte, my children from my first marriage, both of whom had been delivered full term and healthy.

Each boy's first home was a plastic incubator in the Neonatal Intensive Care Unit (NICU) at Crouse Hospital in Syracuse, New York. Because they were so small, they weren't even considered preemies; they were *micro-preemies*.

The boys were in the NICU for months. We had many dark, agonizing days and went to bed many nights wondering if one or both boys would be alive in the morning. Even our good days were full of uncertainty – sitting bedside, rocking sick babies, waiting for answers that didn't always come.

We had hundreds of hours to sit and think about all things, good and bad. The first year included 10 surgeries, dozens of blood transfusions, respiratory distress, the threat of blindness, hundreds of occurrences of interrupted breathing, jaundice, anemia, severe infections and too many needles to mention.

It's amazing what effect this kind of routine has on your emotions and psyche. Do it for a few days and it rubs them raw. Do it for several months and it leaves them raw and exposed. It made me question everything I thought. About everything.

I have a hyperactive brain. I'm not saying it is accomplishing anything, but it certainly never shuts down. I have always soothed my brain by reading a lot – usually 15 to 20 books a year. With the boys in the NICU, I simply stopped reading. I tried a few times, but I felt guilty, as if I should be spending my free time worrying.

Everyone has a story

And then I was given a copy of *On Fire* by John O'Leary. It was the perfect book at the perfect moment. I read it twice the first week I had it.

At age 9, John was playing with fire and was burned on 100 percent of his body. He was given a 1 percent chance to live. *On Fire* is his inspirational story of beating the odds and not just surviving but thriving in life. It cut close to the bone, but it rang true to our situation.

On Fire jump-started my love of reading again, but this time the books I read were all for feeding my brain and my soul. Nothing light – just books about how people had overcome extraordinary hardship, about the wisdom of the ancient Stoics, about faith lost and found.

I started writing down in a journal what I learned and tried relating it back to my life, my family and my work. John O'Leary's words struck a chord:

Introduction

"Owning and celebrating your story will bring new
perspectives and insights to those who hear it, and
will allow you to begin living even more fully."

The more time I spent with *On Fire* and other great books, the
more I wanted to share my story. I'm not a writer, but I started
writing and couldn't stop.

I've read about people who have overcome tremendous tragedy,
hardship, sickness or personal challenges and persevered, only
to say they would not change anything. That never made any
sense to me. It does now. As hard as this experience has been, I
too would not change anything.

This is my story.

THE NIGHT EVERYTHING CHANGED
April 3, 2016

"The boys are here," I said quietly as I returned to the living room, still clutching my phone.

My two friends looked blankly at each other, each hoping the other would know what to say.

"The boys are here? What does that mean?" one asked.

"They couldn't stop the contractions, so they had to deliver."

"Congratulations," the other friend said weakly, almost as a question. We knew very little at that point, but we knew this was not a moment to celebrate.

When our identical twin boys were delivered that night, I was on a golf trip near Palm Beach in Florida, 1,365 long miles from the hospital bed in Syracuse where my wife, Lori, laid, fearful, sore and brave.

The boys, whisked immediately to the NICU, had arrived early.

Fifteen weeks early.

They weighed less than four pounds. Combined.

"I need to get home."

1

Things Don't Always
Go as Expected

When the twins were delivered that night at just 25 weeks, on the fragile cusp of viability, I had no delusions that life was, or would be, a smooth, shady boulevard. I knew all about missed turns, switchbacks and starting over.

I've taken plenty of detours.

At 29, what seemed like the best possible job I could ever hope for was eliminated when my employer merged with a larger bank.

At 43, the ecommerce company I co-founded failed catastrophically, leaving me exhausted, unemployed and broke.

At 50, my first marriage ended in divorce.

Things don't always go as expected. I knew this.

Still, nothing prepared me for all that would follow the boys' arrival. In truth, four new lives started that night. Charlie and Nathan began their amazing fight for survival, and Lori and I climbed aboard a roller coaster of hope, wonder and anguish.

Trying to get out of Florida with spring break in full swing turned into a mean, seemingly unsolvable riddle. My two buddies and I pounded away on our laptops and tablets, looking for flights from Miami, Fort Lauderdale, West Palm Beach, Daytona or

Orlando into any airport in upstate New York.

No seats available.

Sold out.

Please select another itinerary.

We all wondered how I would get home and what I would find at the hospital when I got there. In rushed, anxious phone calls, Lori and the doctors tried to assure me everything would be okay, but what did okay mean in such an extreme medical emergency, with both boys on every imaginable form of life support?

Finally, I landed in Albany late the next afternoon and drove three hours through an April snowstorm to Syracuse.

What awaited me there was the biggest
riddle of all: the future.

Our immediate future was an unfamiliar, alien place.

The NICU is a jolt to your senses. In a room with dozens of sick and weak babies, you find your own child under a plastic dome, with a ridiculous number of wires attached.

The incubators are crammed in tight, with monitors beeping and alarms flashing and chirping endlessly. You interact with your child by opening a door to the incubator and reaching in. You wash your hands a hundred times a day.

Nathan and Charlie were alive, but they faced an incomprehensible uphill battle from Day 1. All my previous life challenges, detours and setbacks seemed trivial in comparison.

DISCUSS WITH YOUR ADVISOR

What life challenges have changed your thinking?

THE FUTURE IS A MOVING TARGET
April 2016

The NICU was the first home our boys ever knew. And in many ways, it became our home too. Tireless, wonderful doctors and nurses became members of our family. On many days, our real house served only as a place to shower, change clothes and try to sleep.

Sleep? We didn't get much. Our minds were too busy trying to sort out the future for the boys, and for ourselves.

We weren't thinking years ahead to day care, trips to Disney or saving for college.

Lori and I dared only to think a week, a day or an hour ahead. We tried to picture a far off future when Charlie would open his eyes, or the results of an important test would come back, or we could hold our babies for even a few minutes.

The future became a moving target, defined completely by whatever medical issue was most urgent – infection, vision, digestion. Only when one hurdle was cleared would we dare look up to find the next.

At birth, the first hurdle was respiration. Because the boys were born so premature, their lungs were completely unprepared for life outside the womb. Machines breathed for them.

Our doctors explained they might be able to boost the development of their lungs with steroids, but – almost every situation came with a but – they would need to wait 10 days before it was safe to try.

Ten days. Ten days seemed like forever.

2

How Did I Get Here?

We like to think of the future as a sequence of decisions, actions and events, strung purposefully together like stepping stones across a creek. One leads reasonably to the next.

Do well in high school.

Get into college.

Earn a degree.

Get a good job.

We are encouraged from an early age to look for and follow these stepping stones, to set goals and actively shape our destiny. We see the future as a logical progression from A to B and onward, something that can be understood and controlled.

That's what we're taught, and I know for some people life unfolds that way. But has that been your experience? My own experience tells me the future is anything but predictable.

Situations change.

Relationships change.

Careers change.

Goals change.

We change.

I am definitely not leading the life I envisioned
20 or even five years ago. This is not the future I
expected or planned for. My life has been full of
surprises, both joyous and harsh.

I'm in my third career. (My fourth, if unemployed and searching counts as a career.) I've been a wealth advisor for more than 15 years now. Though it is not the career I envisioned when I was younger, it's a perfect match for who I am.

I've been married, divorced and remarried.

And now, at 57, I'm raising miracle infant boys with Lori, an incredible woman I hadn't even met five years ago.

I have a beautiful daughter, Charlotte, entering college, and a handsome son, Austin, finishing it. We are also blessed to have in our family Areya, Lori's niece.

Learning as we go

Our blended, multigenerational clan is not a typical family by any means, but like many, it's been shaped by unknowable events. Lori basically became a mom to Areya when Lori's sister died in an accident five years ago. It's not what anyone expected or planned for, but it is what happened. The future controls us more than we control the future.

I chuckle sometimes at the impossible questions we ask young people: "What do you want to be?" or "Where do you expect to be 10 years from now?" Anyone can guess at answers, of course, but for most of us, the future is a mystery to be solved as it happens.

The future takes, but it also gives. Shortly after our wedding, Lori gave me a dozen golf balls imprinted with a perfect message: "SECOND CHANCE."

DISCUSS WITH YOUR ADVISOR

How is your life different today than you expected?

LEARNING BY LIVING
2016

As she started to show, Lori and I saw our lives changing before our eyes. We laughed when words like "minivan" and "double stroller" crept into our conversations. We saw a new life ahead, the thrill of identical twin boys taking on the world.

We never envisioned the boys would be born months ahead of schedule and struggle to survive.

We never could have predicted our lives would revolve for months around a NICU and rely so deeply on the expertise and compassion of doctors and nurses.

We never could have foreseen the love and kindness with which family and friends engulfed us in the confusing, scary and exhausting first months after the boys arrived.

To call the birth of our boys a transformative experience grossly understates it. Lori and I learned so much – about medicine, family, faith, communication, problem solving and patience. And about our own capabilities and weaknesses.

It was like an intensive immersion course in care – both professional healthcare and pure human caring.

I learned so much, and I continue to learn. And to my surprise, I've learned great lessons that help me in my work as a wealth advisor. I'm seeing client situations, both personal and financial, in new ways.

As our boys have grown, so have I.

3

Anyone Can Guess.
But No One Knows.

The investment world has been slow and, in many cases, averse to accept one simple truth: The future is unknowable and unpredictable, playing out a second at a time.

For many generations, the whole idea behind hiring a stockbroker or investment advisor was that a trained expert could look into the future and tell you what to do.

Leveraging his or her superior knowledge of companies and markets, and supported by the additional expertise of researchers, analysts and economists, the broker could confidently tell you which companies and industries were most likely to outperform the market, and when to buy and sell.

The message was clear for individual investors: Financial professionals just knew more and could see into the future in ways that regular people never could. If you were lucky enough to have a broker, his or her recommendations were your best chance for success.

Remember EF Hutton's classic ads?

"My broker's EF Hutton, and EF Hutton says…" The mahogany and leather dining room goes silent, everyone waiting for the sage, omniscient pronouncement of future market events.

Surely one of the great ad campaigns of all time, this perfectly captured Wall Street's premise that financial professionals knew what the future held.

But guess what?

It doesn't work that way.

EF Hutton couldn't foretell stock prices in 1977, and Merrill Lynch and Morningstar can't do it today.

Impossible to predict

I can't tell you if the S&P 500 Index will go up or down tomorrow.

I can't tell you if telecom will outperform banking for the rest of the year.

I can't tell you if gold is ready to surge or plummet. No one can.

Anyone can guess – some will guess right – but no one knows.

Market movements can't be reliably predicted. Especially in the short term.

This is not a grumpy old man's contrarian opinion. This is fact, supported by decades of academic research. Each year, more data appears showing that simple buy-and-hold investment strategies, on average, beat prediction-driven strategies based on picking stocks and timing the market.

This evidence is slowly getting some coverage in the mainstream media, but in the financial services universe it's old news. Brokers know it. Fund managers know it.

Still, prediction flourishes.

Brokerage firms predict stock price targets.

Analysts predict the performance of specific stocks and sectors through buy and sell recommendations.

Economists predict gross domestic product, interest rates and changes in inflation.

Financial media pundits predict how security prices will react to events like elections, economic reports and natural disasters.

Mutual fund managers predict winners and losers through the stocks they choose to include in their funds.

Brokers predict by picking stocks for their clients.

The business models of all these players rely on prediction of an unknowable future. Whether their predictions are based on proprietary computer models, historical analysis or educated guessing, all these people make money by selling their predictive abilities to others.

All these companies and careers rely on prediction despite all of the empirical evidence showing it's not possible to systematically outperform the market based on prediction.

Here's my favorite business model in the prediction business: A pension fund or other big institutional investor hires five or 10 money managers to apply their predictive skills to invest pieces of the portfolio. The fund then hires one or more consultants to monitor, evaluate and rate the money managers, and to predict which of them should be trusted with the largest pieces of the portfolio next year.

That's right. A predictor is hired to predict which predictors are most likely to predict correctly next year. For the institutional investor, that means fees on top of fees, as all of these experts charge handsomely for their services. And because we know it is not possible to systematically and reliably predict, these fees do nothing but reduce overall return.

In the individual investor realm, you only need to flip on CNBC for a few minutes to see how deeply entrenched prediction is. In almost every segment of the daylong broadcast you'll see pundits boldly dispense plenty of reasons why the market is going to go up tomorrow. Or down. Or, more likely, both.

If you encounter an advisor who bases recommendations for your money on predictions of what is going to happen in coming weeks, months and years, I suggest you find another advisor.

You may be thinking, "If prediction doesn't work, how should I invest my money?" That's the subject of the next chapter.

DISCUSS WITH YOUR ADVISOR

Do you think you can predict future market performance?

Anyone Can Guess. But No One Knows.

MY DREAM JOB, OR SO I THOUGHT
1987

It was the summer of 1987 when my friend Rich McGrath gave me a call. "There's an opening on the trading desk." That was all he needed to say.

The trading desk was the short-term funding desk at Shawmut Bank – my personal holy grail. I jumped at the opportunity and was soon a federal funds trader.

Federal funds are a quirky and fascinating part of the capital markets. Banks with excess cash sell it to other banks that need cash. Most of the trades are for one day. Shawmut always needed cash, so every day we would buy $2 billion from other banks, only to return it the next day and start over.

It was fast-paced, with lots of interesting characters, flashing computer screens and rows of telephones. Just like you see in any movie about Wall Street.

The bank was in the middle of a merger when I went to the trading desk. Eventually, jobs were eliminated, including mine. I followed my boss to another bank, where I managed its $750 million investment portfolio.

I was 29 and was certain I had "made it." Until that bank was purchased and, once again, we were all fired.

I was offered similar jobs elsewhere but turned them down. My heart wasn't in it anymore. Trading had become an uninteresting blur of numbers. I needed an intellectual jolt to reinvigorate my love of the markets.

4

The Market Is Your Friend

Investing, like sports and politics, is often framed as a binary contest. You're either a winner or a loser. You become a winner by being smarter than the next guy – buying gold or computer stocks or international bonds when others think it's time to sell.

It's an appealing model – pick the superior team and rake in the riches. Like being on the right side of the fantasy football standings, it's easy to connect with the idea of winning by outsmarting the market, especially because that's the way the financial services industry has been selling itself for generations.

This win/lose model may be easy to relate to, but it's a terrible premise for managing money. That was Gene Fama's message at a Dimensional Fund Advisors boot camp session I attended in 2002.

Some quick background: Dimensional Fund Advisors is a very large and successful mutual fund company that you've probably never heard of. Its funds are available only through advisors who have been trained and approved by Dimensional.

Because I wanted to be one of those advisors, I flew to California to attend Dimensional's boot camp. Gene Fama was one of the speakers.

A professor at the University of Chicago Booth School of Business and one of the clearest voices in modern investment research,

Professor Fama has a special knack for paring complex quantitative research back to its most poignant lessons. I was all ears.

I knew generally what Fama would be talking about. I knew his research had discredited the idea that the smartest person with the best information could consistently beat the market. I knew he advocated a passive approach, one that avoided stock picking and market timing, two longtime staples of the investment advisory industry.

I knew these things going in. Still, I left the session with a completely new outlook on investing.

Work with, not against, the market

Fama told us there was little chance of consistently and systematically beating the stock market. More important, he told us there was no need to try.

Thinking of the stock market as an enemy to outsmart and outmaneuver, he told us, drives counterproductive behaviors that reduce returns and increase risk.

Traditional thinking says it's possible to identify securities that will outperform, if you know what to look for. Follow these secret steps and you can beat the market. If you are smart and disciplined, you can do it.

Fama said the opposite: The harder you try to beat the market, the more likely you are to fail. And furthermore, there's no need to beat the market. It's not a competition. No one has to lose for you to win. Everyone can win.

The public markets allow you to participate in capitalism. Capitalism provides a positive expected rate of return to you for risking your money. It is your reward for being a provider of capital.

The return is not guaranteed. It's not always positive. It's not always immediate. But the *expected* long-term return, based on the long history of capitalism, is positive and generous.

The expected return of capitalism is there for the taking. You just have to participate. That was my light bulb moment.

I'd never heard anyone express so clearly the idea
that investing could be a friendly collaboration
with the market rather than a never-ending
struggle to outsmart it.

In a field famous for know-it-all, do-it-my-way pundits, Professor Fama was begging us to be humble. You can't predict the future, he told us. You can't forecast stock prices. And most important, you don't need to.

Consider these returns: In the 30 years from 1987 to 2016, a $100,000 investment in large company stocks, with dividends reinvested, would have grown to $1.8 million. Or to $3.4 million if invested in small company stocks.

These gains required no clever stock picking, strategic buying and selling or use of complicated options and futures – just the purchase of a diverse bundle of stocks and a trusting, long-term mindset.

Let me emphasize that these gains are the *average* returns for all large and small company stocks over that time frame, not the exceptional returns of top performers. As productivity improved, new markets opened and new technologies were harnessed, patient shareholders were enriched. These gains were possible even though this three-decade time period included major market challenges, from the dot-com bubble and 9/11 to the Great Recession.

Take the returns capitalism offers

Average returns, compounded year after year, can produce exceptional long-term results. Disciplined investors who simply open their palms and humbly accept market-level returns have been well rewarded.

Professor Fama's presentation was a 100-megawatt aha moment for me, allowing ideas I had been exposed to many times before fall into place like the solution to an intricate puzzle. It was the kind of gratifying moment where you want to stand on your chair and wave your arms over your head. (I didn't do that.)

What I heard that day and in subsequent training put behind me forever any attempt to pick stocks or time the market. It helped me develop a belief system about investing, the needs of individual investors and how I could help my clients meet their goals. It was a big day.

Professor Fama has never sought public fame, but it's possible you've heard his name. He won the Nobel Prize in Economics in 2013.

DISCUSS WITH YOUR ADVISOR

Are you satisfied to accept the returns the market offers?

The Market Is Your Friend

ONE GIANT WRONG GUESS
2000

Before the dot-com bubble was a bubble, it was an exciting revolution. Entire industries were being disrupted and reengineered to take advantage of the possibilities of Internet technology.

In the late 1990s, I co-founded a fast-growing ecommerce startup in Boston, a company eventually backed by more than $45 million in venture capital money.

The venture capital guys were the best and brightest, with huge bankrolls. Their faith – and big investment – in our vision only reinforced our great expectations.

When I saw venture capital pouring into another ecommerce business, eToys, I was intrigued. When eToys went public, I wanted in.

And I got in. I moved a lot of my IRA out of diversified mutual funds and dropped it into this one exciting – but unproven and unprofitable – company.

eToys' potential was irresistible. I couldn't talk myself out of it. Following the lead of the venture capital investors, I felt I was smarter than the market. I was sure the $60 per share I paid was a bargain. I knew little about the company's acute cash flow problems, and didn't really care.

I was convinced this was a stock headed for $300. Buying it didn't feel like a gamble; it felt like a smart move for my future.

However, eToys stock didn't go to $300.

It went to zero. Forever.

5

One Stock Is Never Enough

Everybody wants to hit it rich on the next Apple, a stock that doubled in value. And doubled again. And again. And again. And a couple more times. Good luck with that.

It is possible to make an insane amount of money in the stock market if you find the one right stock at the right time. Apple went from a dollar a share to a hundred dollars a share in less than a decade. It's possible.

It's also possible to turn a lonely 10-dollar chip into a thousand dollars at a craps table at The Mirage in Las Vegas. And about as likely.

To hit a jackpot on a single stock, you not only have to be lucky in choosing the stock, you also need to be lucky about when you buy it. You have to see the greatness in the stock before everyone else does.

Apple made a big splash in the mid-1980s with the Macintosh, but it did not make big profits. Apple's stock price stumbled along in the low single digits for 23 years before it finally started going up and up and up in 2004, around the release of iTunes.

It's easy to see now why Apple became one of the world's most valuable companies, but it wasn't at all obvious in 2004. No one struck a giant gong back then to signal it was time to buy. In fact, there was no hint then that Apple would be so dominant in transforming the music business and later get into the phone business and completely transform that industry as well.

The iPad, App Store, Apple Watch – these were not even glimmers on the horizon in 2004.

Yes, buying Apple in 2004 was a great idea that would have made you a tremendous fortune. But few investors were lucky enough to pull it off.

Nonetheless, we can dream.

I was dreaming when I redirected my IRA from mutual funds composed of thousands of companies to the stock of a single ecommerce company.

Working in the exploding ecommerce field myself, I saw eToys as an easy way to double down on the opportunity. I felt like I was on a pretty obvious path to wealth.

Unless, of course, both companies failed.

Which they did.

In less than two years, both companies collapsed, hemorrhaging money too fast to recover. That left me out of work and my IRA empty. I had to borrow money to keep my family afloat.

I could calculate how much my IRA would be worth today if I had just left it in diversified mutual funds. I could, but I won't, because the number would ruin an otherwise lovely day.

Having learned a tough lesson the hard way, I feel no need to be too subtle with the message here:

DIVERSIFYING IS THE SMARTEST AND EASIEST THING ANY INVESTOR CAN DO.

Spreading your money across many stocks takes the worst-case scenario – a complete and permanent loss – completely out of the picture. Any single company can go bankrupt, but a hundred companies in different industries and at different stages of maturity will never fail at the same time.

Diversification has been called the only free lunch in investing because it so dramatically reduces risk and can be accomplished so easily.

How important is diversification? Consider this research finding by Hendrik Bessembinder, a finance professor at Arizona State University, who studied all U.S. stocks over the past 90 years: Over the period 1926 to 2015, a mere 4 percent of stocks accounted for *all* of the net returns of the U.S. equity market. The other 96 percent delivered nothing or had negative returns.

The most common result for any single stock was a complete loss.

This is the reality of capitalism – many companies fail and a few generate exceptional returns. Unless you were lucky enough to pick those rare stocks with decades of high returns, your performance would be dismal. But if you owned *all* of the studied stocks, you would have turned a thousand dollars into millions.

Diversification is easy

Owning a few mutual funds hitches your wagon to hundreds of horses. Some of the horses will be stronger than others. A few may fail. But your fate will never rely on the heroic performance of any single horse to get you across the plains.

The advantages of diversification are well known. Still, I encounter many investors who keep far too much of their wealth in a single company's stock.

In truth, it's pretty easy to end up with too much of your net worth in one company. You may earn stock as compensation in your job, or receive stock as a gift or inheritance.

Getting stock from an employer or loved one can create an emotional attachment; selling the stock can feel like a betrayal. But no matter where the stock comes from, having too much in one company is a needless risk. If that one company goes the way of Enron, Lehman Brothers or eToys, your loyalty will quickly turn to regret.

Unfortunately, I had to live through my mistake with eToys to get diversification into my belief system. I learned this lesson loudly and clearly so you don't need to. Make sure your portfolio is well diversified.

DISCUSS WITH YOUR ADVISOR

Do you have concentrated holdings in any individual stocks?

One Stock Is Never Enough

A VOCABULARY ALL OUR OWN
1987

I spent my early career in the institutional money management business. It was a fast-paced, stimulating work environment with its own language and customs.

As a federal funds trader, I traded *nickels* and *dimes*. Nickels were $5 million and dimes were $10 million. *Fifteen-one-five* meant 15. The *one-five* was used to make sure no one thought you were saying *fifty*, which, of course, was *fifty-five-oh*.

The phones would ring off the hook when the *Fed was in*, meaning the Federal Reserve Bank was undertaking open market operations. Everyone hated a *DK*, or "don't know," because it meant the buyer or seller could not settle the trade.

I usually purchased about $2 billion a day in federal funds, and some days it came down to the wire as the markets were closing. If I was short $500 million, I'd call funds brokers and simply say *"Lite 500"* and then hang up. No time for small talk.

As a bond portfolio manager, I would often ask a broker to *soft circle* a bond. That meant I was interested in buying it, but I hadn't made up my mind yet. I would *hit it* to take off the soft circle and buy the bond.

I bought mortgage-backed securities that were known only as *Freddies* or *Fannies*. Most of the brokers selling the bonds would beg for a *tick*, or an extra 1/32 in price.

To an outsider, it probably all sounded like gibberish. Some of the jargon was meant to increase precision. Most of it was used because it was fun and made us feel important.

6

The Language of Personal Finance

I meet a lot of people that have made mistakes with their money. Often the mistakes happen because they don't understand the basics of investing, or jargon gets in the way.

There is a quote attributed to Albert Einstein that is probably paraphrased but is commonly given as "Everything should be made as simple as possible, but no simpler." I think that is very applicable to people and their money.

This chapter is a quick primer in the basic concepts and language of money management.

Stocks

When you buy shares of stock in a company, you become an *owner*.

Because publicly traded companies have millions, or billions, of shares outstanding, each share represents a very small ownership stake, but you are still an owner. As an owner, your return will be tied to how well the company does. The value of your holding is affected by movements in the stock price and by any dividends paid by the company to shareholders.

You can buy stocks in individual companies or through a stock mutual fund.

Stocks are also referred to as *equity* investments, or *equities*.

Bonds

When you buy a bond, you become a *lender*.

You are lending money to the bond issuer – which may be a company, a municipality, a government agency, the U.S. government or another entity. The issuer pays you interest on a regular schedule and then, at maturity, repays the loan by returning the original investment, or *principal*.

Because you receive predetermined interest payments, bonds are often referred to as *fixed-income* securities.

Cash

Cash is another way of saying *savings*.

Cash is short-term, safe and simple and should involve no risk in getting your money back. Cash includes bank money market accounts, high-quality money market mutual funds or short-term certificates of deposit (CDs).

We all need money readily available for a rainy day to meet some specific short-term need, such as tuition payments, or as a set-aside for unforeseen expenses, like new tires on the car or a leak in the roof.

The trade-off for the convenience and safety of cash is that it produces no growth and earns little or no interest.

Markets

Stock markets are organized exchanges that trade publicly held securities. The New York Stock Exchange (NYSE) is the world's largest stock exchange. The NYSE dates back to 1792, when five securities were traded in an outdoor exchange on Wall Street in New York City. In 2016, the World Federation of Exchanges reported more than $340 billion in daily stock market activity on 64 regulated exchanges around the world.

When you hear someone mention how the "markets" are doing, they are usually talking about the stock market in general or one of the major stock indexes, like the Dow Jones Industrial Average or the S&P 500 Index. This is a useful shorthand reference, but if you own a diversified portfolio of stock mutual funds, your performance may vary from these two benchmark indexes.

There is no centralized exchange for bonds like there is for stocks. Bonds trade between dealers in what is known as the *over-the-counter (OTC) market.* This makes it much harder to track the daily movements of bond prices or to verify the price of an individual bond trade.

Stock prices

Markets allow people to buy and sell stocks. A trade is a voluntary transaction between two willing parties who agree on a price to complete a transaction. They do not have to agree on why they think the price is right; they just have to agree to a price they are both happy with.

The huge volume of daily transactions allows all interested parties – from retail investors to university endowments – to take all available information about a company, and anything else they think is important, and arrive at a market price. The future is uncertain, but prices adjust accordingly.

This doesn't mean that a price is always "right" – there's no way to judge that. But investors can accept the market price as the best estimate of actual value. This is why prices can be volatile in the short term. New information and people's collective reactions to it drive the constant movement of stock prices.

Over the long term, the movement of a single company's stock price is a reflection of how successful or unsuccessful the company has been. The stock market as a whole is an aggregation of all these individual company successes and failures.

This discussion of stock prices reminds me of an experiment I ran at work, trying to test the idea that, collectively, a group is smarter than individuals.

I put a big jar of jelly beans in the break room of the 80-person accounting firm I'm associated with. Over several days, the accountants and clerical staff of the firm posted their guesses of the number of jelly beans in the jar. The closest guess won the jar and its contents. The results were remarkable:

- The lowest guess was 200.
- The highest guess was 5,834.
- The average of all guesses was 1,014.03.
- The actual total was 1,013!

The collective wisdom of the group was phenomenally accurate, even though many of the individual guesses were way off. Together, the group was smarter than the smartest people in the group.

Bond prices

Bond prices fluctuate due primarily to changes in interest rates. Once a bond has been issued, its market value – the price you could expect to get if you wanted to sell it to another investor – moves in the opposite direction of market interest rates.

Here's why. Let's say you own a bond that pays 5 percent interest per year. If the interest rate offered on new bonds of similar length and quality is 7 percent, the attractiveness of your 5 percent bond falls and so does its price in the bond market.

It is important to remember you can hold your bond to maturity and get your entire principal paid back, regardless of any market interest rate movements.

Historically, bond prices have fluctuated much less than stock prices have.

Market index

An index is a measure of something. Financial market indexes are used to measure the change in one part of a market or *asset class*, such as stocks, bonds or cash. A good example of a stock market index is the S&P 500 Index, which tracks the return of 500 large U.S. companies.

Risk and return

Most people are familiar with the phrase "Risk and return are related," but what does it mean?

In free market capitalism, no one would choose high-risk investments if low-risk and high-risk investments had the same expected returns. Investors need to be compensated for taking the higher level of risk. That is, they must see the potential for a higher return in a higher risk investment in order to choose it over a lower risk alternative.

To get a feel for the historic relationship between risk and return, we can examine returns of broad asset classes over many decades. I will use market data going back to June 1927. This covers a long period with positive and negative events both in this country and abroad, including the Great Depression, recessions, growing economies, wars and innovation.

Annual Returns from June 1927 to December 2016

One-Month U.S. Treasury Bills (cash)	3.4%
Long-Term U.S. Government Bonds	5.5%
Large Company Stocks	9.6%
Small Company Stocks	12.2%

It is easy to see the long-term relationship between risk and return with this historic data. Riskier assets like stocks have had higher returns. Cash, the least risky asset class, has had the lowest return.

This makes logical sense if you think of your money market account (cash) in comparison to an investment in a stock mutual fund.

If you put a dollar in your money market account, you know how much will be there tomorrow, the day after tomorrow and a year from now. If you put a dollar in a stock mutual fund, you have no idea what it will be worth tomorrow or at any point in the future. You need to be compensated for that uncertainty or you would never consider holding stocks.

It is important to remember that these are historic returns, not what you should expect for any given year in the future. No one, and I mean no one, has a crystal ball that sees into the future. No one can predict returns.

This data is not meant to entice you to invest all your money in small company stocks, with their high expected return. Doing so would put your money at relatively high risk; this may not be right for you. Instead, use these returns as a guide, an indicator of risk and return relationships and a checkpoint against what people promise you.

No one can say what returns will be for the next 89 years, but I am comfortable believing the general risk and return relationships will be similar.

Inflation

Inflation is an increase in the price of things we buy, often referred to as our *cost of living*.

Inflation is most apparent in the cost of everyday goods. For instance, according to the U.S. Department of Labor, a one-pound loaf of white bread cost approximately 59 cents in 1988. That same loaf of bread cost $1.42 in 2013. In 25 years, the price of bread increased 83 cents or 140 percent.

Inflation affects your investments the same way it affects your ability to buy goods and services. Let's look at the returns shown above after factoring in the impact of inflation, which averaged 3.0 percent during this period.

Annual Returns June 1927 to December 2016 – Net of Inflation

One-Month U.S. Treasury Bills (cash)	0.4%
Long-Term U.S. Government Bonds	2.4%
Large Company Stocks	6.5%
Small Company Stocks	9.0%

While the return pattern is the same – stocks have the highest and cash the lowest – this data shows how your *real* return (the return you keep after inflation) is lower than your *nominal* return (the return before inflation). This is called *inflation risk*.

Although inflation is often ignored in the short term, its cumulative impact can greatly diminish purchasing power. Inflation reduces all investment returns but can make it especially risky to hold large amounts of cash. Money stashed under the mattress or in a low-interest savings account for a long period of time will most likely lose much of its purchasing power.

While inflation has historically averaged about 3 percent annually, it ran as high as 18 percent in the 1940s and exceeded 10 percent in the 1970s.

Again, investment performance can vary widely year to year, so use these figures as a general guideline about the relationship of risk and return. There is no crystal ball to predict future returns.

Bull and bear markets

Market returns are anything but consistent and even. Any graph of stock performance, for example, will be a very jagged line with lots of peaks and troughs.

When peaks are tall enough, they're called *bull markets*. Deep troughs are *bear markets*. Both are normal events, but investors tend to react much more strongly to bear markets.

Bear markets can be scary. They generally start without warning and offer no hints about how long and low they will go.

If you define a bear market as a 15 percent decline, there have been 14 bear markets in the S&P 500 Index since 1950. On average, they've produced losses of about 30 percent and lasted about a year each.

And even in years when a full-blown bear never appears, the stock market is always up and down. Short-term losses of 5 or 10 percent are the rule, not the exception.

During down markets, it's easy to lose confidence in investments, especially when the media is screaming that it is time to sell and that the "smart" money is getting out of the market. Many individual investors react by doing just that. They sell their stocks, preferring to sit on the sidelines until things improve.

Selling after prices fall may provide some emotional relief, but it's typically a bad move financially. Waiting for prices to recover means buying back in at a high price after selling at a low one – the exact opposite of how you make money in investing.

I understand why people panic and leave the market. They let fear take over and fail to consider that even with all the down moves we have experienced in the past, the indisputably long-term direction of the market is up.

Panic is a natural instinct but can be costly. Always remember that every time someone sells, someone else buys. The buyers are probably the investors who are thinking long- not short-term.

Asset allocation

Asset allocation is how you divide your portfolio between cash, stocks and bonds. Given the data above, it is pretty obvious that this decision will affect your long-term rate of return and the volatility of your portfolio.

Asset allocations are not "good" or "bad," but there is an appropriate asset allocation for you, based on your unique set of circumstances.

Rules of thumb for asset allocation related to age or other generic factors lack any insight into your personal situation; avoid them.

Mutual funds

Whether you invest in stocks or bonds, you will have to decide between individual securities and mutual funds.

A mutual fund is an investment vehicle that allows investors to pool their money to purchase investment securities. The advantages of a mutual fund are diversification across a large number of holdings, liquidity, convenience and, generally, lower costs than buying individual securities.

Mutual funds are priced daily after the markets close. The price of a mutual fund fluctuates based on the value of securities held in the fund.

If the underlying holdings pay interest or dividends, or if any of the fund holdings are sold, there may be income tax consequences to the fund holders.

Fund investors pay management fees, known as an *expense ratio*, to the mutual fund managers. These cover the fund managers' advisory fees and administrative costs. Some funds also charge a fee to buy or sell the fund; avoid these.

By the end of the book, I think you will see
why I favor stock mutual funds over picking and
choosing individual stocks.

ETFs

ETFs, or exchange-traded funds, are similar to mutual funds in that they are a pool of investments. They are different from mutual funds because they trade all day long like an individual stock. The price of an ETF is determined like a stock, where a buyer and seller agree upon a price. They can trade above or below the total value of the underlying securities.

Active versus passive investing

Mutual funds and ETFs have one of two investment management styles – active or passive.

Active management is the so-called "art" of stock picking and market timing in an attempt to beat the market. Active portfolio managers are *speculating* on market movements.

Passive management is the *science* of buying large parts of the market (asset classes) to obtain the return of that part of the market. This means the fund manager is not trying to pick individual companies or to time when to move your money in and out of the market. Managers of passive funds accept that they can't foresee the future. If they can capture the returns of the market, and thus participate in capitalism, they are happy.

Passive funds come in various flavors. The best known are *index funds*, which try to mimic as closely as possible specific indexes. Other types of passive funds include *asset class funds*, *structured asset class funds*, or *evidence-based funds*.

DISCUSS WITH YOUR ADVISOR

Do you know how much you are holding in cash, stocks
and bonds, and why?

NUMBERS
2016

I have always been fascinated by numbers. I have wonderful memories of Dad taking me to his office and letting me play on the big, crank-handle Burroughs adding machine. I would punch in numbers and pull the handle until the tape was 10 feet long.

Once a month, I got to help Dad balance his checkbook. I loved sorting all the checks into numerical order and reading the dollar amounts to him. We had shared pride when he announced that the numbers were in balance.

High school brought the magical logic and equations of algebra and geometry. My grades were always high in math and low in everything else. At St. Bonaventure University, I majored in finance and minored in economics. I did the same in business school.

As an institutional money manager, I enjoyed the math of running a bond portfolio. Using modified duration to measure the sensitivity of a bond's price to interest rate movements was second nature to me. I'm sure others would find it terribly boring.

I find linear regression models to be a great way to understand the asset allocation of an investment portfolio. The 3,000 random scenarios of a Monte Carlo analysis make me smile.

I love numbers. But when I learned that *babies born at 25 weeks have a 50 to 80 percent chance of survival*, I realized how inadequate numbers can be in conveying information.

7

Risk Is Not a Number

It's impossible to talk about any element of investing without eventually discussing risk. It's as fundamental to investing as calories are to food. Unfortunately, most conversations about risk miss the mark.

How risky is your portfolio? It's a good question, but can you get a good answer?

The financial services industry, I would argue, does a terrible job of communicating risk to individual investors. More often than not, analysts go straight to the numbers to quantify the risk level of a security or portfolio.

Standard deviation is the magic number for risk. It measures how much returns vary from year to year. Do returns jump around from year to year, or do they always come in near the average? More variation means a higher standard deviation, which means more risk.

Standard deviation is a great statistic. However, if you're a normal person with a career and a family and a dog or a cat, it means almost nothing.

I'm all for using data to answer questions. But unless you have an unusual affinity for statistics, calculating risk as standard deviation won't be of much use to you.

For instance, if I tell you the standard deviation for a particular mutual fund is 5 percent, does that mean it's risky or safe? For most people, it means neither; it's just a number that says nothing at all.

I advocate a completely different approach to talking about risk.

Getting personal

I propose that when you think about risk, you are really thinking about the bad things that would happen if you didn't meet your goals. In investing, you're thinking of the risk of financial distress for you or your family if things don't go well.

Ultimately, risk boils down to one monumental make-or-break question: Will I run out of money late in life?

If we look at risk from this perspective – the possibility of running out of money someday or having to drastically reduce your standard of living – it completely changes the discussion.

Whereas a statistic like standard deviation means almost nothing in personal terms, the idea of relying solely on a small Social Security check to survive is supremely personal. Running out of money presents real, unavoidable implications about how you will secure housing, food, healthcare and other necessities of life.

This perspective on risk is about the *investor* – not about the stock, bond or portfolio. As a spouse, parent or grandparent, you surely don't care about the prospects for a certain mutual fund. But you care immensely about maintaining your own financial independence and protecting the financial future of your family.

My goal in talking about risk is to help clients understand their exposure to the worst-case scenario of running out of money, as well as other financial fears they may have. I discuss how spending and investing decisions increase or decrease that exposure.

I often have to run some quantitative models to do this, but the numbers are there for reference, not as the primary subject of the conversation.

If you work with a wealth advisor, be sure when the topic of risk comes up that the conversation focuses on *your* risk, not solely on statistical measures related to your holdings. The discussion should be goal focused, not market focused.

While we were in the NICU, the doctors sometimes would turn to numbers to discuss options and risks. A treatment option was historically effective for about 70 percent of patients. A medicine had a 60 percent success rate.

I absorbed these numbers but couldn't translate them into anything very useful. Even when I learned that babies born at 25 weeks had a 50 to 80 percent chance of survival, the 20 to 50 percent chance of failure seemed overwhelmingly high, knowing failure meant death. I simply could not connect the numbers to anything I understood.

I see now why presenting investment risk in numerical terms is so unhelpful for many investors: When you're dealing with gut-level fears, numbers don't mean much. Anything less than 100 percent certainty of success sounds like a huge risk.

Too safe can be risky too

Investors sometimes ask for portfolios with "as little risk as possible." This sounds prudent, but it can be a terrible idea. A portfolio with extremely low risk means a portfolio with extremely low expected return. Think of a passbook savings account.

Without accepting some risk, a super-cautious investor is likely to earn so little in return that he or she will not even keep up with inflation. Every year, his or her portfolio has less, not more, purchasing power.

My colleague Larry Swedroe has written in his many books that your risk level should depend on your ability, willingness and need to take risk. Your discussion of risk with an advisor should include all three.

DISCUSS WITH YOUR ADVISOR

How do you define risk?

Risk Is Not a Number

THESE ARE THE ONLY CHOICES?
May 2016

Nathan and Charlie faced dozens of minor and major health issues, including a condition called patent ductus arteriosus (PDA).

PDA is a heart problem that causes abnormal blood flow between two major arteries connected to the heart. The problem is caused by a blood vessel (the ductus arteriosus) that is supposed to close just before birth.

This closure is a regular occurrence for full-term babies but is a missed step in preemies. It must close to allow normal blood flow. Charlie's blood vessel closed on its own within a few days of birth. Nathan's did not.

For Nathan, we were presented with three options: waiting, medication or surgery. The prescribed medication had a very high probability of closing the blood vessel but also had a potential side effect of creating a hole in his intestine.

This was not an easy decision to make. After much thought, the medicine was prescribed. It worked. The blood vessel closed.

About a week later, Lori and I were sleeping when the phone rang. We were told that something was severely wrong with Nathan and that we needed to get to the NICU as soon as possible. In the dead of night, half asleep and scared to death, we arrived at the NICU.

We were told that Nathan had indeed developed a hole in his intestine. The surgeon arrived to give us our alternatives.

"You can do nothing and Nathan will most certainly die. Or I can operate and try to repair the hole, but if anything goes wrong during surgery, Nathan will die. What would you like to do?"

Lori and I looked at each other and cried. How does anyone make that decision?

8

Why Financial Decisions
Are So Hard

Have you ever noticed how mentally tired you sometimes get at the supermarket? Do your eyes glaze over at the freezer full of ice cream choices? Do your home decorating projects take forever because you can't decide what you want?

If you struggle with decisions, I'm here to tell you it's not your fault. We are simply not wired very well for today's world and the complex decisions we need to make.

Our brains have been evolving for about 7 million years, but we Homo sapiens have been around for only about 150,000 years. A 500-page book about brain evolution would devote only the last 11 pages to our big and powerful Homo sapiens brains.

Most of our gray matter evolution took place when we were hunter-gatherers, when our needs and desires were relatively simple and survival-driven. We needed to find food, avoid becoming some predator's food, stay warm and reproduce.

When our primitive selves saw a shadow in the grass, our brain told us to run and climb a tree. It was fast, intuitive, gut-level thinking. Seeking immediate safety was smarter than pondering whether it was a lion, a squirrel or a breeze moving the grass. We were wired to see patterns, think short-term and jump to conclusions.

This type of fast thinking is ingrained in our brain. It operates on autopilot. You have no sense of voluntary control over it. If someone asks you what 2 + 2 is, it comes to you automatically, without effort. You could answer the question if you were sitting in a quiet place or driving your car in rush-hour traffic during a downpour.

But what happens if someone asks you to solve 17 x 28?

You automatically slow down. You know you could get to the answer easily with pencil and paper, but to solve it in your head you would have to break it down into smaller problems and think about holding the numbers in your memory. You can almost feel your brain grinding.

This is not the kind of problem most of us could solve while driving in rainy, rush-hour traffic. If possible, we would postpone our effort on this until we had the time and attention to solve it. Better yet, we would try to get along without solving the problem at all.

Your two brains

This is our amazing two-system brain as described by Nobel Prize winner Daniel Kahneman in his book *Thinking, Fast and Slow*. It's fascinating and I recommend it.

He labeled the fast, feeling brain as System 1 and the analytical, logical brain as System 2.

System 1 is designed to jump to conclusions. ("It's a lion! Run!") System 2 is slower, deliberative, more logical and analytical. ("We should build our hut near a source of water and the hunting grounds but not too close to where the elephants congregate at night.")

System 1 does most of the day-to-day work, with System 2 normally in low-effort mode to conserve energy. System 1 makes suggestions to System 2 in the form of impressions, intuitions, intentions and feelings. System 2 is sort of lazy, so it usually takes the suggestions of System 1 and things run pretty smoothly. You trust your intuitions and emotions and act on them.

This is how our brains evolved. We're programmed to act on instinct and solve simple problems on the fly. When the problem is complicated or vague, or we have too many choices, we tend to get bogged down or fall back on what is familiar.

Instead of fully pondering the spectrum of ice cream choices, trying to juggle all the brands, flavors, prices and calorie counts, we pick the one we had last time. If we can avoid a complex decision, we will.

We're wired primarily for System 1 thinking but live in an increasingly System 2 world.

We want shortcuts

How does our two-system brain deal with financial decision making? I think it's fair to say most people struggle with it. We avoid, ignore and procrastinate. We look for ways to bypass decisions that require research, evaluation of alternate strategies or messy calculations.

Investors are often led to mistakes by their System 1 brains. System 1 is always ready to take over when System 2 lacks the time and energy to grind out an answer. This evolutionary bias plays out in several familiar ways.

We see patterns that may not be there

Pattern recognition helped our ancestors understand that there were seasons for planting and seasons for harvesting, that dark clouds meant rain and that a movement in the grass might be a lion.

We instinctively look for patterns in investing. Unfortunately, it's easy to see a pattern that isn't there. If stock prices go up three days in a row, it feels like a trend that will continue. If the industrial equipment sector does well in two consecutive summers, surely it is a smart buy for the third summer.

Pattern recognition causes investors to chase "hot" money managers or market sectors the way a gambler bets on "hot" dice. Other investors believe charts of market data hold patterns that can predict price movements even when there is no evidence this is true. The entire financial news business is built on forcing disparate events into cause-and-effect relationships. ("Stocks plummeted today on a rise in oil prices…")

Investing technology allows us to track and parse security prices like never before. Fancy graphs with colorful lines trace minute-by-minute price movements. System 1 wants to see patterns in all of this and often does, leading to instinctive, not rational, investment choices.

We overvalue surprises

Thousands of years ago, it was very important for our brains to recognize things that were unusual. Perceiving and reacting to surprises – a predator in camp or a fast-rising river – helped keep us alive. System 1 saved us from danger.

We're wired to handle modern-day surprises in the same way, but retreating from every event outside the norm ensures terrible investment results. If you got out of the stock market every time the market fell unexpectedly or a terrorist event occurred or a major political crisis unfolded, you'd be out of the market more than in it, and you wouldn't participate in the long-term benefits of capitalism.

System 1 lives moment by moment. It's not looking 30 years ahead to retirement. We must force System 2 to get involved in longer-term investing decisions.

We trust our emotions

Making investment decisions would not be so difficult and intimidating if we had perfect information and a clear picture of what the future holds. But we have neither. When System 1 doesn't have all the facts, it fills in the holes with emotions.

Investing can be very emotional. Especially in times of uncertainty, financial decisions can be derailed by fear, greed, panic and impatience. Even a positive emotion like confidence can lead to some poor choices.

I'd be the last person to advocate a life without emotions, but in making long-term investing decisions it's important to understand how strongly emotions can push us further and further away from the System 2 rationality we need.

A defense against System 1

An Investment Policy Statement (IPS) is a written document that acts as a guide for what you want your money to do for you and those you love.

You can think of the IPS as a sort of rule book or operating manual for your investments. It is based on your unique set of hopes, dreams, goals and fears. The policy statement needs to be in writing and should be signed by you and your advisor. It should include your target asset allocation (mix between stocks and bonds), and it should be updated on a periodic basis as your life evolves.

When your System 1 brain wants to respond to patterns, surprises and emotions, the IPS is the rational, rules-based guidepost that reminds you of what you are trying to do and the plan you have committed to. The IPS is developed with the kind of methodical System 2 thinking you need when System 1 is doing everything it can to control your behavior.

I don't think it is realistic to believe we can automatically become disciplined, non-emotional investors by simply writing a policy statement, but we have to start somewhere. An IPS might mollify your temperament and help you stick to your plan when emotions take over in good markets (greed and envy) and bad markets (fear and panic).

What did we do in the NICU?

"You can do nothing and Nathan will most certainly die. Or I can operate and try to repair the hole, but if anything goes wrong during surgery, Nathan will die. What would you like to do?"

Lori and I looked at each other and cried. How does anyone make that decision?

We were lucky. Standing next to us was a NICU doctor we affectionately referred to as "the smartest woman alive." She is everything you would want in a doctor: blisteringly smart, compassionate, wise, dedicated, tough and kind. We looked at her and shrugged our shoulders. Neither one of us could speak.

"Surgery," she said. "Nathan is a tough boy. He will do just fine. Have the surgery."

Surgery it was.

We were lucky to have someone at our side to help us make a decision with an appropriate balance of logic and emotion when we were operating in the most panicked levels of System 1 thinking.

By the way, the surgery worked.

DISCUSS WITH YOUR ADVISOR

How do you make important financial decisions?

LET ME SHOW YOU ANOTHER GRAPH
2014

A couple of years ago, my son Austin invited me to give a talk on investing to his fraternity brothers at Rochester Institute of Technology (RIT). Fortunately, he got the really smart gene that skips generations, and has excelled in the software engineering program at RIT.

I was thrilled to accept the invitation. I knew I'd be speaking with a bunch of super-bright future millionaires and was excited to get them off on the right foot on personal finance.

Preparing for the talk, I fired up PowerPoint and started pulling all sorts of slides from presentations I had done over the years, especially client meetings.

I had a graph that used the past 90 years of historical data to show the relative performance of stocks versus bonds.

And another that compared big stocks versus small stocks.

And another for diversified portfolios versus single stocks.

And another that showed how mutual funds that outperform one year tend to do poorly the next.

And so on.

These were all slides I knew inside out. I chose them because they illustrated important lessons through research and evidence. They presented facts, not theories. I loved these slides.

And the fraternity brothers loved them too.

9

How We Say Things Matters

Why is it so hard for so many experts to explain things in regular English? Wouldn't it be great if every time you needed the help of a mechanic, arborist, lawnmower repair guy or lawyer, you could understand what he or she was saying?

Does this sound familiar? Your refrigerator or other modern convenience starts acting up. You call a certified professional to come to the rescue. He or she makes a diagnosis and calmly explains the problem.

Ten words into the explanation, you're lost. The part names, meter readings and error codes mean nothing to you. You give up and just wait for the estimated cost to fix whatever needs fixing.

This communication disconnect serves no one. We all understand this problem and all know the answer – use normal, simple language! Still, when it comes time to make a recommendation, most experts fall back on what they know best – the complicated technical details.

I do it too.

Investing is technical. When I studied finance in school, and as I learned more in my early career managing investments for a bank, the goal was always to master the technicalities, the things that, frankly, only an expert cares about.

That means jargon, acronyms, data, percentiles, regression to the mean. And graphs. Graphs galore. So it was only natural, I suppose, that as a wealth advisor I've often tried to educate clients using the same technical, detailed, quantitative tools.

That is, tools only a bunch of RIT hotshots can relate to.

Austin and his pals loved my quant-rich PowerPoint deck. A mix of math majors, engineers and future tech moguls, they live on a daily diet of graphs and equations. They see the world in bell curves, ratios and probabilities.

These young men with no assets to invest – meaning no immediate need for most of what I was preaching – nodded appreciatively with each new slide. And they asked great questions, the kind of questions I hoped to, but rarely did, get from prospective clients.

The RIT guys seemed much more interested in investing than do most of the investors I meet with – some of whom look at me like I'm the well-meaning appliance repairman trying to teach them the science of refrigeration.

Which makes sense. My clients and prospective clients are, for the most part, not scientists. They're not engineers. They're not bankers. They're entrepreneurs, executives, parents and grandparents. They don't think in charts and graphs. They think in families, careers, relationships and dreams.

No wonder the room often goes pretty quiet when I get into charts and graphs in client meetings. The traditional language of finance is too technical and too detached from everyday life.

I'm not the only financial professional dealing with this issue. As a whole, the financial services industry spends an inordinate amount of time, energy and money crafting answers to questions most investors are not asking.

What finance is best at answering:	What people really care about:
What is the expected return of this portfolio?	Will I run out of money?
Is the risk level of this portfolio proportionate to its expected return?	If I die, will my loved ones be okay?

Speak the right language

This disconnect is not news to me; I've continually tweaked and questioned how to best communicate investment ideas to people with no interest in becoming experts.

It's a work in progress. As one of the positive results of a very trying experience, my time in the NICU helped put the topic in better perspective.

Neonatal medicine is, of course, far more technical than investing, but I was consistently impressed with the medical staff's ability to describe what was going on with the boys without drifting too far into the scientific weeds.

We asked simple, layman's questions and, for the most part, got answers we could understand:

"Why can't Nathan keep down this formula?"

"We think he's having trouble handling the fat content. So we'll try some other options with different kinds of fat."

An exchange like this didn't turn us into pediatric dietitians. We couldn't name the specific lipids giving him trouble. But we understood what was going on. We didn't have to ask for any vocabulary definitions.

We didn't need a degree in biology or chemistry to follow the discussion.

Moreover, the doctors didn't hand us articles from the *Journal of Pediatrics* to peruse in our spare time or send us links to poignant research on fats and emulsions on the *New England Journal of Medicine* website. In fact, they specifically told us not to look for this kind of information.

They stuck to ideas we could follow and were patient when we asked more questions.

Old habits are hard to break, but I definitely learned a lot about communication from the boys' doctors and nurses. In my client meetings, I'm striving for more plain-English discussion and fewer graphs, definitions and research papers.

DISCUSS WITH YOUR ADVISOR

What would you like your advisor to explain –
in plain English?

How We Say Things Matters

I WANTED TO GO HOME
2010

I've been involved with the Syracuse Rescue Mission for many years. It's a wonderful organization dedicated to ending hunger and homelessness in Central New York. It helps people pull themselves out of addiction, abuse and despair. It's an incredible honor to be part of it.

Some years ago, although I thought I knew pretty much all there was to know about the Rescue Mission, I had an experience there that changed me forever.

Along with the other board members, I was invited to check into the overnight shelter. I welcomed the opportunity to see how the center functioned from the viewpoint of its clients.

Of course it was just a daytime field trip. The shelter was empty and we were all in our clean, pressed business clothes. I was given a blanket and a bed assignment.

Once inside, I immediately became uncomfortable. I found myself in a completely unfamiliar world. Everything about the place was so far from anything I had experienced in my own life.

I had a strong and emotional sensation. I wanted to go home. Not home to my wife and kids and comfortable living room, but home-home. I wanted to see my parents. I wanted to thank them for giving me a life where I never had to wonder where I would sleep or get a warm meal or try to get through a day without taking drugs. I wanted to crawl into my twin bed back in Cortland, New York, and be safe.

After uneasily making my assigned bed, I was asked to role-play with a counselor. That's when everything went off the rails.

10

Understanding Gratitude

I've always thought of myself as a thankful person. I have so many things to be thankful for, and I am. But life is an amazing teacher, and I keep learning how many things I've taken for granted.

The goal of the role play at the Rescue Mission was to challenge board members like me to think about the men who normally stayed in the overnight shelter not as headcount statistics but as individuals trying to get through difficult lives one day or one night at a time.

The role play made it personal. Very personal. I was given the role of a 16-year-old runaway boy who had been physically abused by his mother's boyfriend.

"Tell me about growing up. What has your life been like?" the counselor asked calmly.

I shifted nervously in my chair, rolling responses around in my head. Trying to find something that fit the scenario I was given.

But no words came out.

"Tell me about your family," she urged me gently.

I felt my heart pounding, but still no words. I could not put myself in that place. I didn't know anything about abuse or running away or living on the streets.

My life has been blessed

My life had been just the opposite. When I was 16, my biggest concern was making the varsity basketball team. When I argued with my parents, it was about things like mowing the lawn or being allowed to use the family car to drive around with my friends.

There were no bullies, abusers or predators in my world. No juvenile court or eviction notices. No sleeping on sidewalks or foraging in dumpsters. No standing in line for meals.

An abused runaway? I couldn't even pretend. I just sat there. I didn't say a word. I choked up and shook my head weakly, staring at the wall behind the counselor.

This was one of those learning moments you can't forget even if you wanted to.

<hr />

Only by trying to imagine the helplessness of someone else was I able to see all the help and advantages that I'd had my whole life.

<hr />

It was the first time I could see how lucky I was to have been born to my parents, and how all the gratitude I had tried to express to them and others could never be enough.

Growing up, I lived in a safe, comfortable home in a safe, comfortable town, Cortland. My parents loved and protected me. They made sure I got a good education. I've never been hungry. I've had good friends my whole life.

I now live in Skaneateles, another town that is, if anything, even safer and more comfortable than my hometown. My older children are awesome. Lori is wonderful. Our niece, Areya, adds another welcome smile to the household. And now we have two incredible little boys to cherish and spoil.

A circle of family and friends

In times of need, people have always been there. When the twins arrived so early and weak, hundreds of people rushed to our aid. Word spread and love poured in.

Meals appeared on the front porch. I found a stroller in the driveway one morning. College friends I'd not been in touch with for decades sent daily text messages of hope and encouragement.

And prayers. I couldn't count the number of people who prayed for us. Even total strangers, moved by the struggles of these tiny babies, took time in their days to send their anonymous love.

How do you begin to be thankful enough for all of that?

To be honest, it's not been easy or natural to accept so much kindness. I've always tried to be a little bit invisible, preferring to give help rather than receive it.

When the boys were about 10 weeks old, one of my friends pulled me aside. "I need a list of things you need," he said. "People want to know."

This buddy had appointed himself press secretary for my family soon after the births, knowing we were too overwhelmed to keep everyone up to date on the progress and setbacks of the boys. Whenever I shared news with him, he blasted it to friends from Boston to Boulder.

"Everyone keeps asking me what you need," he said. "So what do you need?"

I tried to explain we didn't need much. I told him the meals our friends were supplying made a huge difference, relieving us of cooking and shopping chores. Beyond that, I didn't want anyone to get caught in our emotional roller coaster ride. "Not really anything," I said.

"Let me put this another way," he said, smiling. "This isn't about you. People want to help. They need to. They care about you and want to *do something*. So I'm gonna need a list."

The need to give

He was right. People do care and do want to help. I've always known this. I love to help people, whether at work or in the neighborhood. Delivering holiday meals for the Rescue Mission to families around the area has been one of the most rewarding things I've ever done.

What I've come to fully appreciate only more recently, however, is that for someone to give help, someone else must receive it.

This receiving part has been trickier for me. But I'm getting there.

With cards and prayers and meals and high chairs and diapers pouring in, I realize that gratefully accepting the support of others is as big a part of being human as offering it. And not welcoming help and encouragement can be perceived like returning a gift to the sender, unopened.

I had a sweet conversation with a lifelong family friend who was sending adorable outfits to Charlie and Nathan every couple of weeks. "You've been so generous. I hope you know you don't need to send more," I told her.

"Oh, I know that," she replied. "But I never had kids, so I'm going to spoil them like they were mine, and that's that."

I send a newsletter out to clients periodically, a mix of financial news and other items I think people might be interested in.

When Charlie, at five months old, finally joined Lori, Nathan and me at home, I decided to put a short blurb about the boys in the newsletter.

For most of my clients, this was the first they'd heard about our situation. It was just a couple of short paragraphs describing the medical and emotional journey we'd been on in the NICU. It felt good to let people know, but I didn't expect much reaction.

In the week that followed, I heard from more clients about that brief piece than I had in response to 15 years of prior newsletters combined. They offered support and thanked me for sharing. Once again, I was amazed by the outpouring of care and concern.

Having had so much support from others makes it so satisfying to be in a career where I can help others reach their goals. It's like a big circle of help and gratitude, a cycle that never stops.

DISCUSS WITH YOUR ADVISOR

What are you grateful for?

SOME ASSETS ARE LIABILITIES
2016

After getting separated and divorced, I slid way down the housing scale. When I moved out so the kids could continue to live in the family home with their mother, I became a house sitter for a friend whose home was on the market. I later moved to a scraggly rental property.

When the landlord decided to sell the rental, I moved again, buying a "historic" fixer-upper a few blocks from the kids.

By historic I mean old and crooked. The original structure was built not long after the Civil War, and it had been added on to multiple times over the many decades since. The end result was a cute little place with low ceilings (my six-foot-six son had to duck through every doorway), a bent and twisted porch, and a second floor banked like a racing oval.

Even with its many flaws, it was home. I saw it as a place to hang my hat, and I looked forward to the various renovation projects (some more than others).

Immediately after closing, the kids and I painted the entire interior. Austin and I pulled off the old porch and started a long and laborious rebuild. I gutted the upstairs bathroom. Later, I did a basic remodel of the kitchen.

It was all as messy, expensive and rewarding as the home remodeling shows on TV.

Amid all these projects, I met Lori. When we got married and she moved in, it was clear we'd eventually need a bigger home. A year later, with twins on the way, we knew it was time to sell.

However, no one would buy.

11

The American Dream?

A job. A family. A house. For many, these are the unquestioned badges of success and happiness. Owning your own home is front and center in the iconic American Dream. But is homeownership truly dreamy?

Let's all agree: Owning a home is emotionally appealing. It's your very own place to make memories, decorate to your taste and take refuge from the rest of the world. Most renters anxiously await the day they can finally call a place their own.

Financially, however, owning a home may not be as wonderful as it sounds. Here are a few realities of homeownership that often fly under the radar.

Owning is expensive

Even if you get a great deal on the purchase of your home, you will probably spend far more living in it than you expect. Between utilities, insurance, property taxes and general upkeep, your monthly ownership budget will add up quickly.

Eventually, you'll face significant repair costs too. Roofs leak. Appliances wear out. Big trees need removal. Foundations crack. These are normal and necessary expenses, but because they may arise when you are least prepared to pay for them, they can strain family finances.

Renting can be frustrating and unsatisfying in many ways, but it has one great benefit – when the dishwasher dies, you call the landlord.

Houses don't always appreciate

Many argue that a home is the best investment you can make, and if you buy the right house at the right time for the right price, that can be true. But it may not be.

Remember, a home is a depreciating asset. Unlike a fine wine, it doesn't get more valuable just because it gets older. In fact, even the best-built home in the neighborhood will slowly degrade over time. Thanks to weather and normal wear and tear, money must be spent just to maintain a home's original condition and value.

There's no assurance a property will increase in value. Some real estate markets do experience booms that drive prices quickly higher, but others are slow to rise. And struggling neighborhoods often see declining prices.

Anyone expecting to make a significant profit on
the sale of a home needs good timing and good
luck, neither of which can be guaranteed.

The mortgage interest deduction is not so valuable

Many homebuyers are motivated by the reduction in taxes that mortgage interest earns them. Or that's how they see it, anyway.

The actual benefit is less than it may seem.

Mortgage interest is a deduction, not a tax credit. You do not get a one-dollar break for every dollar you pay in interest. The amount of the tax break is based on your tax bracket.

Furthermore, to get the tax benefit, you have to itemize your deductions. Many homeowners receive no tax break at all because their deductions do not add up to more than the standard deduction. Homeowners who do itemize deductions get only pennies on the dollar for mortgage interest paid.

Homes are illiquid

Liquidity is a measure of how quickly you can turn an asset into cash at a fair price. For convenience and control of your finances, liquidity in any investment is a big plus.

Stocks are highly liquid. With today's sophisticated electronic stock markets, it's a routine transaction to sell a hundred shares of Ford at the prevailing market price.

More specialized assets are less liquid. Selling a gold coin will take some time and effort, as you must find someone who is willing to pay what you consider a fair price. You may have to lower your price considerably to sell it quickly.

Selling a home can take months. Finding a buyer that places appropriate value on the location, layout and condition of a home is generally so difficult that sellers hire professionals to do it for them, and pay handsomely for the help.

Even with a real estate agent involved, some homes are difficult to sell. The sloping second floor of my place ultimately scared away all the potential buyers who liked the rest of the house. It sat on the market for a year, even after we had moved to a larger home better suited to our newly extended family.

With little other choice, we eventually had to hire a structural engineer to find the cause of the sagging floors and a contractor to correct it. (Apparently, when the staircase to the second floor was widened decades ago, key floor joists were removed and not replaced. Ugh.) The repair allowed us to sell the house, but we did not recoup the cost.

Homes are indivisible

There's another element of illiquidity that erodes the financial dreaminess of homeownership. If you need to raise cash – say, to send a child to college – you can't just sell your basement or garage. You have to sell the whole property and find a new place to live.

In many cases, the only way to get some of your equity out of a home is to take a home equity loan…in other words, pay a bank interest to let you use some of the value of your illiquid asset.

I'm not trying to discourage anyone from buying a home. Lori and I love the newer, larger home we've purchased. I can't wait to chase the boys around the back yard. But it's important to make all investment decisions with eyes fully open to the financial side of the story, not just emotions. Buy a house you love, but don't count on it for financial benefit.

DISCUSS WITH YOUR ADVISOR

Do you view your house as a home, an investment, or both?

The American Dream?

NEVER TRUST A PREEMIE
July 2016

The boys had survived three months. They had endured emergencies and scares of every kind. We started letting ourselves think everything would be okay. Common mistake. As they say in the NICU, "Never trust a preemie."

It was a glorious Saturday morning in July. The nurses and doctors coaxed us to go home and enjoy the day. We did.

We were home for a few hours when Lori's cell phone rang. As the caller ID flashed "NICU," our hearts stopped. The voice on the other end said calmly, "We don't know what is wrong with Charlie, but you need to get here as quickly as possible." Just thinking about that still makes me weak in the knees.

The 30-minute drive seemed like three hours (even though I ran red lights and crossed double yellow lines every chance I got). By the time we got there, they had determined Charlie had a hole in his intestine. He would need emergency surgery right away.

The surgery was successful, but because the contents of his intestines had spilled into his body, he became septic. Sepsis is the result of an infection, and causes drastic changes in the body. It can be dangerous and potentially life threatening.

After a sleepless night, I was back in the NICU early the next morning. Charlie was in terrible shape. His tiny body was swollen to what seemed like double size. Too weak to move, he couldn't even open his eyes. How could he possibly survive this?

I stood over him, completely overwhelmed. The weight of three months of worrying came crashing down on me.

12

Embracing Our Internal Struggles

Emotions can sometimes turn our worlds inside out and upside down, but where would we be without them? We'd have no idea what was important, when to ask for help, or how to think about the future.

On that Monday in the NICU, I lost it. I cried so hard I couldn't talk. My shoulders shook. I gasped and slobbered. I came apart at the seams.

I had no reason to think I would ever stop sobbing.

Then, seemingly out of nowhere, Nurse Beth walked up to me and gave me a huge hug. She dried my eyes with a cloth diaper and said, "It's about time you fell apart. I was starting to worry that you would try and keep all this inside you forever."

With that small gesture of kindness and a couple of sentences, she saved the day. She changed my life. She changed me.

I grew up thinking crying was a sign of weakness. I was raised in a Greatest Generation household. Mom, and especially Dad, instilled in my brother, Michael, and me a deep sense of personal responsibility and accountability.

In our house, we were expected to stand on our own two feet. Dad did not raise us to be complainers or whiners, and certainly not criers.

I held on to that for my entire adult life. It was easier for me to stifle the emotion than to let it show.

Beth gave me permission to show my vulnerable side. I had been hiding it, pushing it down whenever it tried to rise.

It was a relief. With my façade of composure shattered and splattered across the NICU floor, I entered a more honest, more authentic world.

Yes, I was scared.

Yes, I was exhausted.

Yes, I was vulnerable.

And yes, it was okay to let it show.

Money and emotion

While we may want to think otherwise, money can be very emotional. Money is important to how we live and what we can do for ourselves and our loved ones. When people talk about serious money issues, tears are not unusual.

As proof of money's emotional importance, misunderstandings about it can lead to terrible arguments and ruin relationships.

Once in a while, clients cry when they come to talk to me about their finances. While I don't always know exactly how to respond, I don't discourage the tears. Tears are a sure sign I'm hearing the unedited, unvarnished truth about whatever problem is on their mind.

Often the problems that trigger tears are not even what most people would think of as problems. I have some clients, often older and usually women, who have accumulated significant wealth by being good savers and thrifty spenders. But still they worry.

They have far more money than they will need to live comfortably, but worrying about money is simply rooted in their belief systems. Because they cannot see with certainty into the future, they worry that they will not just run low on money but actually become bag ladies.

That's how they say it, and they're serious. With far more than enough money safely invested, they worry they will someday be homeless, living out of a shopping cart.

That's real, raw emotion that's holding them back from a happy life. It causes some to hoard money, miss out on the benefits of a prosperous life and essentially sabotage their later years. Others invest with such a low level of risk (and low return) it limits how much is left to pass on as a legacy to future generations.

Only by letting those emotions out can situations like these be fully discussed and addressed.

The conversation can start with two simple questions:

1. What do you hope will happen?
2. What do you fear will happen?

An honest discussion of these two questions, with or without tears, helps put a lot of important issues into perspective.

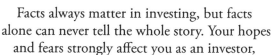

Facts always matter in investing, but facts
alone can never tell the whole story. Your hopes
and fears strongly affect you as an investor,
often not for the better.

Attitudes about money are usually more complicated than they seem and are often tied to experiences or lessons learned early in life. It is very common for clients, even those who are in their 60s or 70s, to talk about how their parents' spoken and unspoken attitudes about money still influence their outlook many decades later.

As another example playing out today, many young people whose first investments were ravaged in the Great Recession got out of the stock market and are reluctant to return, even though the U.S. stock market fully recovered all the losses and has reached much higher highs since the end of the crisis. Fear holds them back.

Acknowledge your emotions

In a battle between emotions and facts, facts face a big disadvantage. But ultimately, when people can be honest about their emotions, they're more likely to make rational decisions and find a sense of calm about finances. As an advisor, I encourage clients to acknowledge and discuss the emotions that can complicate and undermine financial decisions.

Unfortunately, repressing or avoiding emotions can be a natural response to uncertainty. My belief system was that crying was a weakness. Nurse Beth opened my eyes to the benefit of being honest with myself and others. Keeping all that fear and anxiety inside is dangerous and exhausting.

I now can see that by allowing my emotions an outlet, I am simply making a commitment to live a fuller, more honest life.

I guess everyone needs a Nurse Beth in his or her life. I'm so thankful I found mine on that tearful Monday morning.

DISCUSS WITH YOUR ADVISOR

What do you hope will happen?

What do you fear will happen?

I TURNED OFF THE TV
AND NOTHING HAPPENED
2016

When the twins were born, Lori and I went into an instinctive parental survival mode, focusing all our time and attention on their health and safety.

Outside of my time at work, I spent almost every waking minute at the hospital or making preparations for the day they would – hopefully – come home. I was singularly, obsessively focused.

I immediately shed activities not related to this survival mission. Things like social life, exercise and recreation went out the window. So intent on getting the boys to eat and gain weight, I lost interest in my own meals.

I also went 158 days without any news. I just turned it all off. With all attention on medical status, there wasn't any more room in my brain for politics, terrorism or Syrian refugees.

Apparently, there was a harsh and divisive presidential election campaign going on, but I didn't know much about it. I was getting my daily news not from anchormen and reporters but from doctors and nurses in the NICU.

The headlines that mattered to me involved poop and pee, not presidential debates and email servers.

And you know what? During and after my extended media blackout, the sun continued to rise. My work carried on as normal. My clients were fine. The markets continued to work. Life went on.

13

The News Won't Help You

Whoever has the best access to current news gains a significant advantage as an investor. Because information is power. This notion seems almost self-evident. But is it really true? Does consumption of news help investors?

Something amazing has happened in my lifetime. News coverage has evolved from a soggy morning newspaper and 30 minutes of Walter Cronkite to a dozen 24/7 cable news channels supplemented by online media outlets, social media, podcasts and blogs, all competing for eyeballs and ad revenue.

News is big business, and the line between entertainment and information has been thoroughly smudged, if not erased altogether. With so much time and space to fill, news coverage has become more specialized, sensationalized, partisan and repetitive.

It's also faster. News that once might have taken hours or days to reach you is now vibrating on your phone in a matter of minutes.

The acceleration and expansion of the news cycle sound like a boon for investors, providing more information on which to base decisions. But I'd argue the opposite is true.

Everything I see tells me that the more investors try to use what they see and hear in the news to improve their investment results, the worse they do.

Here's why news is so unhelpful:

It's old

No matter how close you sit to your computer monitor, you cannot systematically receive – and act on – news before other interested investors can. Just try to get a trade in ahead of institutional supercomputers when the new jobless claims numbers or Federal Reserve minutes are released. You can't do it. By the time you're ready to press Buy or Sell, the news is already old and reflected in security prices.

It's amplified

News sells only if it's dramatic and surprising. In the battle for audience share, unbiased and reasoned perspective has been the biggest casualty. Today's headlines are crafted to provoke, not enlighten. Facts are expressed in sensational, often misleading ways. Seemingly any story, no matter how trivial, can now be packaged as "breaking news." Bill Gates has a nice way of framing this: "Headlines…are what mislead you because bad news is a headline, and gradual improvement is not."

It's repetitive

Filling an endless news cycle means relentless repetition. One story about a small interest rate hike will barely register in your consciousness, but hearing that same story repeated every 20 minutes all day long can make it feel like an impending disaster.

It's opinion

Much of what we see on "news" outlets is commentary. This is especially true in the financial press, where scores of pundits and analysts present theories as to why certain stocks are priced too high or too low. Though these predictions may sound convincing and factual, they're still just opinions.

It's emotional

Perhaps worst of all, news is now designed to trigger emotional responses. A glowing headline about a great GDP number excites investors. A gloom-and-doom story about job losses scares them. When emotions take over, we know investors make poor decisions – jumping in and out of the market, picking hot stocks that turn cold, and basing long-term decisions on short-term information.

Taken together, these characteristics make news coverage a real threat to smart investing. News can breed unnecessary fear or unreasonable optimism, both of which can lead to buying and selling the wrong things at the wrong times.

News can be informative and entertaining. It may
help you in other areas of your life, but in investing,
it's more likely to hurt than help.

I see the impact of news stories on investor psyches all the time. Clients call me, worried about how the latest political or economic storyline will affect them. It's not idle worry; it's real concern, because we've all been trained to take the news seriously.

I welcome these calls, as they provide an opportunity to reinforce the basics of modern investing – diversify, buy and hold for the long term, and stop trying to outsmart the market. But it can be difficult to convince an investor that the news crisis du jour should just be ignored. We've been trained to give the news credence it often does not deserve.

The drama in the NICU gave me an excuse to turn off the news. Now I wish I had done it years ago. In the quiet and calm of a media-free life, I realized how we are brainwashed to think every single news event, celebrity sighting and political tweet matters.

When I turned off the news, I found I had more time and less distraction. I also had a feeling of empowerment. I gave myself permission to say "I don't care" to the latest poll numbers, the shocking Kardashian photos and the tired partisan bickering in Washington.

My experience tells me that turning off the news will help you be a better and calmer investor. And a happier person in general. Give it a try.

DISCUSS WITH YOUR ADVISOR

Do you ever want to change your investments based on news headlines?

The News Won't Help You

BABY STEPS
2016

There are no healthy babies in the NICU. It's an accidental community of infants born too early, too small or in need of special care.

The twins' neighbors in the NICU were suffering from severe lung issues, aggressive infections and bowel blockages.

Some had heart defects, jaundice or high blood pressure.

Some wouldn't eat. Some wouldn't poop. Others wailed and shook from addictions inherited from their mothers.

Most, on top of other issues, had compromised immune systems, making them susceptible to new infections and illnesses.

It was sick children, tubes, bandages and monitors wherever you looked. But even surrounded by families dealing with all of these heartbreaking illnesses, we soon came to a scary realization. We didn't have the sickest baby in the unit; we had the two sickest babies.

After our first week or so in the hospital, our friends started asking us the natural question – when can the boys get out and come home?

That question hadn't even reached our radar screen. (We'd answer it with a hopeful smile and "Probably a couple of months," but we didn't know.) The milestone we thought about was getting to the point where Charlie and Nathan were no longer the sickest babies in the ward.

The boys' journey to good health and a normal childhood looked a million miles long in those early days. So we had to think of it as many, many shorter trips all strung together and intertwined.

14

One Milestone at a Time

I was talking to a marketing guy one day. He asked me why someone hires a financial advisor. "It's like a toothache," I told him. "You may not want to go to the dentist, but when a toothache gets bad enough and won't go away, you go. It's the same in my business."

Financial toothaches take many forms. You wonder how you will pay for your daughter's college. Or you're getting divorced and need to start over financially. Or your small business needs a cash infusion. Or you paid a crazy amount in taxes this year and need to make changes.

A toothache can be positive too – you've sold your business and don't know what to do with the money. Or an inheritance puts you in a new financial situation. Or you've retired and want to turn your 401(k) holdings into many years of comfort and travel.

When I meet with someone for the first time, he or she will often express some embarrassment or regret about not seeking professional help sooner.

I completely understand that, and I try to reassure people on three key points.

First, procrastination is normal. It's far more common to delay and ignore financial planning than to be proactive and prepared.

Things like retirement planning are firmly anchored on the back burner in most American households.

Second, procrastination often makes the situation worse, but it rarely makes it fatal. Doing anything – even late – is better than doing nothing, and with some thought and attention, any financial situation can be improved.

> I think for most clients, the relief of finally taking steps in the right direction more than offsets the regret of doing too little for too long.

Finally, not everything needs to be fixed immediately. Financial planning is often an incremental process where we tackle one element at a time, taking small steps over several years to address investments, paying for college, retirement planning, estate planning, insurance and other pieces of the financial puzzle.

If reading this reminds you of your own procrastination on financial planning, I encourage you to take the first step and seek out the help of a wealth advisor. You may feel the same kind of relief we felt when we no longer had the sickest kids in the NICU.

DISCUSS WITH YOUR ADVISOR

What one financial situation do you want to work on first?

One Milestone at a Time

NOW WHAT?
2015

It happens in every family, but when it happens in your own, it can be upsetting, confusing and frightening. I'm talking about the point when aging parents need more care, help and attention due to declining health.

We encountered this situation in my family about a year before the twins were born. When my father, who for several years had been the primary driver and food shopper for himself and my mother, fell and ended up in the hospital, we had to make some changes.

Based on rehab results and medical advice, we soon all came to the same conclusion – my folks needed to move out of their home of 40 years and into an assisted living facility that offered a wide range of conveniences and services, including 24/7 medical care and all their meals.

To say this was an emotional experience for all involved would be an understatement. No matter how rationally we considered the realities of their situation, it was difficult to accept a new chapter was beginning, whether we were ready or not.

It was discouraging to see my father, always an active, independent guy and a daily swimmer, in the hospital after falling. It was equally hard to accept that my mother needed care he could no longer be certain to provide.

Feeling a little bit like the survivors of a flood that had washed away all we had known and taken for granted for decades, we had to quickly make decisions and plans about a new and different future.

15

New Chapters in Old Age

Things don't always go as you expect. This is true for you, your spouse and your kids. It's also true for your parents as they get older. Because the health situations of seniors can change so quickly, adjustments in living situations often must be made with little notice.

My parents enjoyed many, many years of excellent health – far more than average. They watched as most of their friends declined; many passed away. But time catches up with everyone eventually.

When my mother's faculties started to fade, Dad was able to take up most of the slack. He's always been a take-charge person, so he took charge of the household and kept things running pretty smoothly without much help.

But when he – the healthy one – ended up in the hospital, suddenly we realized that we didn't have a plan to cover that scenario. My brother and I and our families went into scramble mode. In fairly short order, we got an assisted living arrangement set up, but until we did, we were all in a frazzled state of uncertainty.

> With my parents' health and welfare on the line,
> the last thing we wanted to do was to make quick
> decisions, but we had to.

We didn't have time to drive all over upstate New York to tour assisted living facilities. We didn't have time to price shop. We needed a safe place for Mom with care options that matched her needs. We needed it to be comfortable for Dad too. And we needed it fast.

My advice for others is to start thinking and talking about possible scenarios for your parents before issues arise – ideally long before, while everyone is physically and mentally healthy and there's no pressure to make any immediate decisions.

Expect surprises

Discuss plans based on what you expect to happen and also on situations that seem less likely, such as the healthier partner becoming ill or incapacitated.

Discuss temporary situations, like one partner being in the hospital for a week or so, and permanent situations, like needing help with everyday tasks such as meals, transportation and personal care.

Consider future living options – from in-law suites to assisted living communities. Visit facilities, if possible.

Discuss how much care you or other family members are willing or able to provide, as well as your options for professional caregivers. Discuss the costs of different care arrangements and who will pay them.

Deal with the topics no one wants to deal with, such as when it is time to give up the car keys.

And prepare for the day when your parents can't, or no longer want to, handle their finances. It's pretty common for one spouse to manage most or all of the money responsibilities in a household. If that person is suddenly unable to do so, it can be a panicked, disorganized transition for whoever has to take over.

If your parents are getting older, I suggest you spend some time together and put together a financial lifeboat kit that includes as much of this information as possible:

- Where are bank accounts?
- What bills must be paid monthly and annually – mortgage, utilities, credit cards, etc.?
- What bills are paid with checks versus online?
- What are the passwords for online accounts that need attention?
- What insurance policies are in effect? Who can tell you more about them?
- Is a long-term care policy in place? Do you know what it covers and what conditions activate it to pay benefits? (It can be trickier than you think.)
- Are there trusted advisors who may be able to provide help or information – an accountant, attorney or investment advisor?
- Is there enough money (between Social Security, pension and investments) to support current and future expenses?
- Are powers of attorney active at all relevant financial institutions so money decisions can be made by those best able to do so?

Assembling this information can feel like a nuisance for all involved, and your parents may not even want to discuss turning over control of their finances. Nonetheless, preparing for future changes is important, and it's so much easier to do before an emergency strikes.

As we found in my family, it's impossible to fully anticipate what's ahead for your parents (or for yourself, for that matter); however, an open mind and open dialogue can only help the process. The discussions may be difficult to initiate but can lead to wonderful conversations.

DISCUSS WITH YOUR ADVISOR

Have you discussed with your parents how they want their financial and healthcare matters handled if they can't help themselves?

New Chapters in Old Age

PLEASE DON'T GO ON GOOGLE
2016

Can you remember way back in olden times when the search for an important fact might start with your trusty and dusty World Book Encyclopedia?

If you couldn't find it there, you might have to visit the local library. A dead end there could mean a call to your smartest friend or even a letter to some expert in the field.

Even with all that time and effort invested, coming up empty was a real possibility.

Today, we feel let down if we have to do more than one Google search to find whatever we need. It's pretty remarkable how quickly we can access information. But it's not always ideal.

Google is an amazing resource, but it can be a real problem in the medical field. What you find is often confusing, incomplete or just plain wrong.

If you've ever turned to Google to figure out a mysterious sore spot, unusual rash or nagging stomach issue, you probably discovered in short order that you had a terminal illness. Then when you rushed to your doctor, she explained it was not terminal, was not a disease and would clear up in a couple of days.

Our NICU team implored us, "Please don't go on Google." They warned Lori and me that the information we found was bound to scare and distract more than enlighten.

We did our best to not play Dr. Google, but that was easier said than done. When we strayed, it was never helpful.

16

Too Much Information

Not knowing what's going on can feel very scary. However, thinking that we know what's going on when we don't is usually far more dangerous.

In a previous chapter, I discussed how unhelpful the news media can be for investors. The never-ending news cycle produces stories that often scare or mislead, resulting in emotional – and often costly – investment decisions.

The same warning applies to the Internet, with the added bonus that essentially anyone, anywhere, can post information or opinion on the web. The seemingly coherent advice you discover in a blog post may have been written by someone who knows far less about investing than you do.

Furthermore, much of what you find online is advertising, which we know can never be trusted as complete or impartial.

So what we end up with on the web is a perfect storm of truth, lies, opinions, rumors, marketing hype, exaggeration, rants and just plain crazy theories presented as facts.

Ads are not advice

For instance, I just did a search on this phrase: "best investments for retirees." The first page of results delivered about 18 clickable items, including six ads. Here are some of the subject lines:

- "6 Best Investments for Retirement"
- "Retirees Should Consider These 3 Ultra-Safe, High-Yield Stocks"
- "7 High Return, Low Risk Investments for Retirees"
- "The 6 Best Stock Funds for Retirees in 2017"
- "2017's Best Annuity Rates – From America's #1 Rated Source"

Well, they all sound great, but obviously they can't all be the best investment options for seniors. I'd venture none of them is the best, and some may be terrible choices for any given retiree, as every individual's situation is different. There may even be a Ponzi scheme in there, for all we know.

There's no reliable way for investors to evaluate the suitability of any investment advice or information they find online. Just like in the medical field, the best way to use Google may be to not use it at all.

As soon as we met our NICU doctors, we were certain they knew far more than Google. For starters, they knew Nathan and Charlie. They knew the boys' immediate status, they recognized the seriousness of their challenges, and they saw the subtle, minute-by-minute changes that affected the babies' prognoses.

They also had the benefit of caring for thousands of other preemies before Nathan and Charlie came along. They had seen treatments that worked and trouble areas to watch for. Their approach was both art and science, shaped by experience, research and instinct.

With all that knowledge and context, the doctors offered us a solid basis for trust and eventually for optimism and hope. Google could spit out things for us to read until we turned blue, but it could never provide the context and nuanced perspective our doctors did.

If you give it the opportunity, Google will probably convince you at some point that you are doomed as an investor and offer you a "secret answer" that leads you to extremely counterproductive investment decisions.

I would never equate medical and financial advice, but I will say this: The unbiased perspective of a professional, in medicine, finance or any other field, is so much more valuable than anything you will find on your smartphone.

DISCUSS WITH YOUR ADVISOR

When you have a money question, where do you turn?

YOU CAN'T COME BACK
Summer 2016

On the endless list of things that scared us at the NICU, the boys' persistent habit of not breathing was about the worst. It's a common issue for preemies, but knowing that didn't help.

When the babies stopped breathing, the pulse oximeter monitor activated audio and visual alarms. A hundred straight days of that awful beeping and flashing drove us half crazy. We started hearing the alarms in our sleep. If we heard a similar sound outside the NICU, we would jump to action like Pavlov's dogs.

The nurses did their best to allay our fears. They coached us through the process, explaining what was happening and why it would eventually stop. We learned what to do but never got comfortable with the idea that the boys could stop breathing at any moment.

And then, out of blue, it stopped for Nathan. No more alarms. He started to breathe on his own, all day long. He was getting healthier.

Only one week later, we learned Nathan was scheduled to go to the "zoo" in five days. The zoo is HOME! (No one would be foolish enough to say "home" out loud in the NICU.) We had prayed for months that this day would come, but with it came a whole new level of fear and worry. How could we take this once terribly sick baby (now weighing a whopping three and a half pounds) home?

We had loathed the chirps and beeps. Now we begged the doctors to let us take these awful monitors home. They told us no, that wouldn't be necessary, that we'd be fine.

To top it off, we learned that once a baby is released from the NICU, he can't go back.

17

The Spend-Down

According to the magazine *Scientific American*, more people die coming down Mt. Everest than going up. Apparently, this is true in climbing in general. On the way up, intent on reaching the goal, climbers are focused and energized. On the way down, physically spent and less motivated, they are more prone to mistakes and accidents.

I see a direct parallel here with financial planning. The entire planning industry is based on saving and investing to build a nest egg for retirement – the climb up the mountain. There is very little focus on what happens once you reach that goal. How you adjust your investments and spend your money – the safe trip down the mountain – gets little attention.

The transition from accumulating wealth to spending wealth can be a difficult one. It requires a different mindset and demands that investments play a new role. Because it is new and unfamiliar territory, I feel investors may need at least as much guidance from a wealth advisor in the spend-down phase as during the accumulation period.

Part of the challenge is that once you reach retirement, it's generally not feasible to go back. If you find, for instance, that after 15 years of retirement you're depleting your assets too quickly, it's unlikely you can un-retire and replenish your nest egg.

This was part of our distress when Nathan was discharged from the NICU. Because he could bring in germs or illnesses from the outside world, he could not be readmitted to the NICU. The amazing doctors and nurses we had relied on would no longer be his caregivers. We had to build new skills, learn new systems of care and find our footing in this new phase. Transitions like these are unsettling.

The spend-down phase would be much simpler if you had a foolproof crystal ball.

For instance, if you knew you would live to exactly 85, your spouse would live to exactly 88, you would spend $100,000 a year, inflation would remain constant at 2 percent, your diversified portfolio would return 7 percent every year, you'd never need expensive 24/7 care, and so on, you could easily run the numbers and validate your spend-down plan.

Of course, real life is nothing like that. Life is unpredictable, especially in one's later years.

Spend-down planning must recognize the uncertainties of retirement while using available tools and techniques to maximize your opportunity to live with dignity and independence and to leave the legacy you envision.

Here are some topics to discuss with your wealth advisor as you prepare for and execute your spend-down plan:

Plan optimistically for life expectancy

No matter how sophisticated medical science becomes, it's impossible to know whether a healthy person will remain healthy to age 95 or encounter life-threatening medical issues at 65. According to data from the Social Security Administration, a woman turning 65 today can expect to live to almost 87 (84 for men). An upper-middle-class couple age 65 today has a 43 percent chance that one or both will survive to at least age 95, according to the Society of Actuaries. It's best to plan for a long life, well longer than average. This, of course, means a longer spend-down period.

Be realistic about spending

After a lifetime of being thrifty and saving for retirement, many people find it difficult to start spending for retirement. Some investors want to spend investment income only, not principal, which can lead them to buy high-yield, potentially high-risk investments. A comprehensive long-term cash flow analysis can help you get your arms around what is an appropriate level of spending.

Count on inflation

Although inflation rates have been modest over the past decade, the drain of rising prices over long periods is very significant. Historically, the rise in the Consumer Price Index has averaged about 3 percent. That rate of increase would mean your spending would double in 24 years, the length of retirement for many people. All planning should reflect realistic inflation levels.

Be strategic with Social Security timing

You and your spouse have choices about when you begin taking your Social Security benefits. In general, the longer you wait, the greater your monthly benefit will be. The rules on spousal benefits are complicated; the timing you choose can have a big effect on your benefit amount. It's worth the time to research the topic or discuss it with your advisor.

Control investment costs

Pay close attention to the fees mutual fund managers charge. The *net expense ratio* states the percentage of fund assets paid for operating expenses and management fees. Actively managed funds often charge fees of more than 1 percent. Passively managed funds usually charge much less. These small, consistent savings compound into a big difference over the remainder of your lifetime.

Manage taxes

The most important investment performance measure is your after-tax return – not what you earn but what you keep after taxes. That's what you can spend, save for the future or give away.

What many investors forget is, within some limits, you can control what you pay in taxes. Here are two examples of techniques any investor can use to reduce the bite of taxes.

First is *tax loss harvesting*. This process does what it says: It harvests losses in securities that have declined in value to offset gains in other investments. So if you sell some holdings at a profit, you could sell others at loss. The loss nets out some or all of the gain, reducing the tax due.

The second technique is *asset location*. This means putting the right kind of assets in the right kind of accounts. Because of the differing treatment of capital gains and interest income, you can reduce your taxes by holding stocks in ordinary investment accounts and bonds in tax-deferred accounts.

Holding stocks in taxable accounts, not tax-deferred accounts, also helps position your family for a tax-free step-up in cost basis upon the death of the account holder.

Think multigenerationally

There are many ways to transfer wealth to future generations and to philanthropic causes. Depending on your personal circumstances, it may be beneficial to begin that transfer well before you die. Doing so will mean the beneficiary has access to the funds sooner, and the bite of taxes may be reduced as well.

In the end, your money can go only four places: your own spending, your heirs, charity or the government. Smart planning can make sure more of it goes where you want.

DISCUSS WITH YOUR ADVISOR

Are you confident you will never run out of money?

THANKSGIVING DAY
2016

An amazing thing happened at the Gardner house on November 24, 2016.

Charlie and Nathan were home from the NICU.

Charlotte was home.

Austin was home from RIT.

Areya was home from Ithaca College.

My parents came to dinner.

Lori's parents came to dinner.

We all sat around the same table.

At the same time.

Together.

Life is full of moments to be thankful for.

This one will stick with me forever.

18

The Myth of Normal

Looking around the table, I felt so grateful for our unique and special family. What I saw was a multigenerational extravaganza of strange proportions and juxtapositions, with half-brothers ranging in height from 18 inches to six-foot-six. I loved it.

The traditional family of two parents and 2.1 children still exists. But it now lives next door to families like our Brady Bunch combined unit. And single-parent families. And families with two fathers or two mothers. And grandparents raising the kids. And kids caring for grandparents. And every other nontraditional variation you can imagine.

It's these "unusual" circumstances that give families their character and make a personal relationship with a financial advisor so important.

When I meet with a prospective client, we talk about money and investments, but more importantly, we talk about people. I ask about family members and other loved ones. We often talk about careers, hobbies and health.

The conversation is part of simply getting to know someone. It's also essential to learn about the family before trying to offer any guidance on finances.

Personal finance, it turns out, is very personal. The financial services industry often tries to convince us otherwise.

Can a robot understand you?

An interesting movement has sprung up in wealth management in the past few years: robo-advice.

As the name implies, robo-advice automates many aspects of investing. An investor answers a series of questions on a website and a specialized software package recommends a portfolio "suitable" for his or her needs and tolerance for risk.

The quotation marks around *suitable* reflect my uncertainty about how well an online algorithm can discern and interpret what is right for a specific investor. For the most part, robo-advisors ask questions about money, age and future cash needs, not about family, family businesses, health, philanthropy and other highly personal elements that can and do influence investment strategies.

Take the Gardner clan as an example. Knowing my age, income, when I plan to retire and my general attitude about investment risk leaves out almost everything that is important to me – my atypical family, the commitments I have made to them and my goals for the future. A robot could generate a suggested portfolio, but it could never understand what my life is about.

Just as important, a software package can't sit down with you and calm your nerves when a bear market sets in. It can't respond to your expressions of fear, impatience or uncertainty.

100 minus your age

There's a popular and long-referenced rule of thumb in investing that you should hold progressively less stock and more bonds as you get older. More specifically, if you subtract your age from 100, the rule says, that's the percentage you should hold in stocks.

So a 40-year-old should own 60 percent stocks and 40 percent bonds. A 70-year-old, needing more stability and less risk, should own 30 percent stocks and 70 percent bonds.

It's easy math, and to my thinking, it's pretty much worthless.

This simple equation leaves so much information out that the result, for almost any individual, is meaningless. That's the danger of trying to apply a big, homogenous rule to an extremely heterogeneous population. More often than not, the slipper won't fit.

10 times your salary

How much life insurance do you need? The life insurance industry's rule of thumb is 10 times annual salary for an individual.

It's an easy rule to remember, but I feel it's one that's best forgotten.

For starters, if no one is financially dependent on you, you probably do not need any life insurance at all.

If you do need coverage, the calculation of an appropriate amount is far more personal and complicated than the 10x formula. You need enough coverage to help your survivors maintain a desired standard of living and avoid undue financial stress. If you have children, you might want to provide for their education. You may need to provide for your spouse's retirement.

An appropriate coverage level is influenced by many variables, including marital status, number of dependents, the ability of your spouse to earn a living after your death, the size of your mortgage and other debt, potential education expenses, and many other factors. The 10x number may make sense for a small part of the population, but in most families it will be too high or too low.

An attentive and thoughtful advisor who knows you and understands your family would never use rules so blunt and clumsy to design your financial plan. If you meet an advisor who doesn't ask about you as a person, beware.

DISCUSS WITH YOUR ADVISOR

What is unique about your family?

The Myth of Normal

YOU ARE IN OUR PRAYERS
2016

It started as soon as the boys were born. People reaching out with words of encouragement and kindness. I soon realized nearly everyone I spoke to would repeat the same phrase – "Nathan and Charlie will be in our prayers."

It made me sit up and take notice. While I was raised with faith, I had come to question it in my adult years. I am a right-brained person. Facts and figures for me. If you can't prove it, it can't be real.

But there it was again. One of the guys from my spring golf trip sending me an email: "My mother is praying for your boys. And her prayers are very powerful."

Nurses, doctors, friends, acquaintances. All saying that Nathan and Charlie would be in their prayers.

It was easy to tell these were not empty words. You could see the concern on their faces and hear it in their voices. A nurse told me one morning, "I was up all night praying for Charlie." The dark circles under her eyes verified it.

A nurse practitioner returned from a week's vacation to tell us how she went to the Cathedral Basilica of St. Augustine, Florida, to light a candle and say a prayer for Charlie. On her vacation!

Over the past year, I have witnessed a miracle. Many miracles. Time and again, I have seen two babies overcome life and death odds. It has made me rethink most everything I have believed up to this point, including my faith. If all these people pray for my boys, who am I not to? Who am I not to believe in something bigger?

19

You Gotta Have Faith

Faith: *a strongly held belief.*

I have always had a strongly held belief that capitalism works. As an open-eyed optimist, I always believe the future will be better than the past. My strong faith in the stock market is second nature and unshakable.

As I have begun to rethink my religious faith, it has made me think long and hard about how I talk to my clients. How I always tell them to "have faith," even when all signs are negative. Faith in the stock market is so automatic for me that I never realized how empty those words might sound to other people.

When the boys were in the NICU, we were told to have faith, but it was so hard to believe things would work out okay. It was hard to stay positive day after day when we faced so much bad news, one life-threatening crisis after another.

The bad news was always *so* bad, we greeted any positive news with a grain of salt. And it wasn't just us. In the NICU, you never say your child is having a "great day." NICU superstition requires you simply say, "Things are okay."

Worst-case thinking

I see now that this same thinking is prevalent among many stock market investors. People have a very hard time staying positive – or even neutral – during down stock markets. Bad news is amplified, magnified and memorized. Good news is discounted or ignored altogether.

While most investors take up markets for granted, down markets can cause sleepless nights and stressful days. Down markets feel so much worse than up markets feel good, they just never balance out. Bad always seems stronger. Dark beats light.

In the NICU, it was easy to take every beeping, flashing monitor alarm and extrapolate it into a worst-case scenario. When you watch your child stop breathing, how can you believe the nurse who tells you, "Everything is just fine and this is normal behavior for a preemie"?

I knew faith could only help us. Still, it was hard to have faith in the plan, faith in the doctors, and faith in the uncontrollable, unknowable future.

In one of my darkest hours, a very kind doctor grabbed me by the shoulders, looked me square in my tear-filled eyes and said, very forcefully, "I will get this baby home for you if it is the last thing I do." This wasn't blind faith, wishful thinking or ego. She was expressing her faith. She had complete faith in her team and herself, based on years of experience, knowledge and hard work.

Her faith was also faith in the boys. They were born wanting only to live, preprogrammed by millions of years of evolution to fight and never stop fighting. Our doctor was never going to give up, knowing Nathan and Charlie never would.

During the five months we spent in the NICU,
our faith grew, nourished by our daily experiences
and reinforced by the inexhaustible faith of
our doctors and nurses.

I have been involved with the capital markets most of my adult life. My faith in these markets is unwavering. I know how they work and that our capitalist system is destined to create prosperity and wealth.

But that's not true for most people. They see the markets as big, mysterious and potentially dangerous. They remember bear markets, losses and fear. They forget bear markets end, forget bull markets have created billions of dollars in value for investors, forget the S&P 500 Index has risen from 80 to more than 2,400 in the past 50 years.

I recently read a book that had a fantastic quote from Richard Rohr, a Franciscan priest: "Faith is remembering in the darkness what we have experienced in the light." I thought about this quote often during the summer of 2016. It truly helped me get through some dark hours.

Investors will experience darkness. It's inevitable. But so is light, light that is so much brighter than the darkness is dark. To get from one to the other takes faith.

DISCUSS WITH YOUR ADVISOR

Do you have faith in the markets?

THE OLDEST DAD IN THE ROOM
2016

At some point as you've been reading this book, a thought has probably crossed your mind. You tried not to think it, but you did. It's okay. I understand. We're all friends here.

What you thought was: "Fifty-six is awfully old for a new father. Geez, you'll be 74 when those boys graduate from high school!"

You're right. I'm old for a dad. It's a badge I wear with pride. Most of the parents in the NICU were 20 or 30 years younger. One well-meaning mom greeted me with a reasonable question one evening: "I see you have two grandsons in the NICU. How are they doing?" In her shoes, I probably would have made the same assumption.

Lori and I have to laugh at some of the funny looks we're bound to get as we take our boys out in the world, where most new parents are 26, not 56. (Lori, fortunately, not only is younger than I am but also looks even younger than she is.) Someone's sure to assume on the first day of kindergarten, summer camp, Cub Scouts or soccer practice that I'm the helpful granddad, filling in for the real dad, who's busy at work.

We have to laugh about these prospects, but there is a serious side to the age gap. No one lives forever. According to the actuarial tables, my life expectancy at this point gives me another 24 years or so.

With good behavior, maybe I can add another 10 or even 20 years to the average. But I'm sure to be gone for many years by the time Nathan and Charlie reach my current age.

20

Don't Leave a Legacy of Confusion

How will you be remembered? Your loved ones will certainly remember and cherish your love, kindness and generosity, but will they also face a disorganized mess when they get to the point of settling your affairs?

No one wants to think about dying, but not thinking about it assures that anyone you leave behind will face inconvenience, frustration and possible expense when you do pass away. I strongly encourage you, no matter what your age or health, to take the time to put in place the essential documents that will help your loved ones when they need it most:

- Will
- Durable power of attorney
- Healthcare proxy
- Living will

You'll need and want the help of an estate planning attorney to determine exactly what you need and to create the documents. Your wealth advisor should be involved as well.

Because every situation is unique, I won't try to explain all the details that should be considered as you develop your estate planning documents. But I will offer some advice on how you can help your loved ones by getting organized and staying organized.

Each thing you can cross off this list is one less task for your heirs.

Things

The possessions you accumulate over a lifetime may give you comfort and pleasure, but they may be a big headache for your family after your death.

Even a well-organized and cared-for collection (whether it be cars, coins, antiques, tools, etc.) can be burdensome for heirs to keep and difficult to sell quickly at a fair price.

A disorganized hoard, even if it is valuable, can become a part-time, no-pay job for your children or other heirs.

A good mental exercise to run every few years is to envision all your belongings piled in a big, open space. How much is there? Will anyone want it when you are gone? How much effort will it take to sell? Does anyone in your family know how or where to sell or donate it?

Periodically thinning the herd may help everyone involved. Donating items that you no longer need is a win-win-win for you, your heirs and the recipient of the donation.

Also consider compiling a current inventory of your possessions and having appraisals done on valuable items. This will save some work for your survivors, who may have little insight into the importance or value of your belongings.

Information

Can you condense your life into one small filing cabinet? With so much information now stored forever on the Internet, this goal is more feasible than ever before. Create, clearly label and maintain current files for the following items:

- Real estate – deeds, leases and mortgage information
- All outstanding loans
- Insurance – all types
- Social Security information
- Vehicles – title, registration, and lease or loan information
- Credit cards, including store cards
- Safe deposit box and storage locker locations
- Passwords for online accounts, protected by encryption
- Checking and savings accounts
- Investment accounts, including online accounts
- Recent tax returns and documents needed for your next return
- Pension accounts, IRAs and other retirement accounts
- Employee benefit contacts
- Military discharge papers
- Club memberships and other affiliations that need to be terminated
- Business succession plan documents
- Divorce agreement or adoption papers
- Prenuptial agreements
- Will and living trust documents, including documentation for any assets you have transferred into the trust

Think of this cabinet not as a dumping ground for everything that comes in the mail but rather as a living body of information that changes over time. Review all files once a year and streamline wherever possible, as obsolete items will only confuse and slow down your survivors. Close unused accounts. Switch to online statements where appropriate. Update passwords. Weed out investment statements with no remaining tax consequences. Purge out-of-date insurance policies.

Keep the names of and contact information for all advisors, bankers, insurance agents, employers, etc. in one place for easy reference.

Remember that organizing almost anything on this list is more easily done by you than by your family after you are gone. They will need to find passwords, distinguish current accounts from old ones, furnish death certificates, sign innumerable forms and seek the assistance of many people they have never met. It will be a lot of work.

Wishes

You may have ample opportunity or no opportunity at all to say goodbye to loved ones. If you're not the type to gush your sentiments on a daily basis, consider writing letters to be delivered to your family members upon your death. There are online services that facilitate this, or simply leave letters with your attorney or a trusted friend.

Likewise, if you have preferences for funeral arrangements, discuss them now or put them in writing. This will be a matter of the utmost concern for your family in the period when they are least prepared to deal with it. Leaving instructions will greatly simplify their duties while they grieve.

Your obituary will also be an immediate and difficult task. Keep a file of information you'd like included, or write your own. After all, who knows you better?

Final steps

Your family will be going in circles immediately after your death. It will be a big help if they know the first step they need to take – for instance, contacting your attorney, who can help explain what needs to be done.

You may want to ask this trusted advisor to hold some written instructions to be shared with your family. The guidance and organization will be a big relief to all. Good organization and planning can also head off disputes or disagreements among your loved ones.

Planning for the time when you are gone is nothing you want to do, but it is definitely worth the time and energy it requires. Good preparation is a true gift for those you leave behind.

DISCUSS WITH YOUR ADVISOR

If you died tomorrow, would your heirs know what to do?

THE NICU YODAS
2016

The indoctrination to the NICU assaults your senses. It is an isolated world with its own language, customs, superstitions and rules. It is completely cut off from the normal everyday interactions of career and family life.

You enter the NICU full of fear and trepidation and your defense mechanisms are on high alert. Everything around you is alien, confusing and fragile. You don't know what to do, what to say, even where to stand.

Lori and I surprised ourselves with the strength and resilience we mustered as our boys fought for their lives. But we did not, and could not, make the journey on our own. We needed someone with experience, education, wisdom, intuition and kindness to guide us through this bewildering and life-changing period.

Fortunately, there is a special breed of superheroes at Crouse Hospital who devote their lives not only to the survival of precious babies but also to the comfort and well-being of the parents: the NICU nurses.

Hanging out with a NICU nurse for six straight months is like being with Yoda, the wise and generous two-foot-tall Jedi Master from the *Star Wars* films.

We watched the nurses, learning our way in unknown territory. But they watched us as well, knowing exactly when to intervene with information, encouragement, or a silent, gentle hug.

21

When Work Is Love

"I work here because I get to see miracles happen." The first time I heard one of the nurses say this, referring to Nathan, it took my breath away. I realized how sick he was and how fortunate we were he had survived his latest medical crisis.

"I work here because I get to see miracles happen." When I heard this same statement over and over again from many other nurses, it made me step back and think. It is a statement of such pure joy and love for what they do and for the children they care for.

The nurses feel so intensely about the work they do, there's no limit to their efforts, nothing held in reserve. They take a personal stake in every baby in their care. I don't know how they keep it together, dealing with tiny, suffering infants every day.

We were lucky enough to see this devotion come full circle when Lori and I visited the NICU on the boys' first birthday. We brought cupcakes and two beautiful little boys.

The doctors and nurses got to see the Gardner boys for the first time in seven months. They couldn't hug the boys any tighter.

Here were their little miracles in the flesh. At 13 pounds each, the boys looked like giants compared to the micro-preemies the doctors and nurses had coaxed to health for half a year. The staff saw their hard work and commitment rewarded in those smiling 1-year-old faces.

By that visit, we knew every inch of the NICU, but it reminded me of our first days there, when our guides, the nurses, knew exactly what we needed:

- **Guidance and feedback**. They challenged us to get involved and get our hands dirty. This helped us gain confidence and focused our attention on things we could control.

- **Empathy.** The depth of their empathy was a real learning experience, something I had never been part of before. They cared about our children seemingly as much as we did.

- **Listening.** They were great listeners and very intentional listeners. Not just to the task at hand but also to our fears.

- **Advocacy.** They were tireless advocates for our children and taught us how to be advocates as well.

- **Expectations.** They shaped our expectations. Not false optimism but realistic expectations that grounded us in our true situation.

- **Trust.** Trust is the basis for any successful relationship. The NICU nurses built trust through their words and actions.

They helped on every level. The issues we faced ran the gamut from the practical (how to change a diaper on a two-pound baby hooked up to several different tubes and monitors inside an incubator) to the emotional (how to deal with two extremely sick children every day for half a year) to the medical (how to handle nearly daily decisions on treatments and procedures).

Above and beyond all else, they helped us face our fears that the boys might not make it home.

I wish I were a gifted enough writer to adequately put into words the depth of our appreciation, gratitude and love for the NICU nurses. All I know is they saved us.

My professional guides

Guides appear when we need them throughout our lives – coaches, teachers, friends, colleagues. I am lucky to have had some wonderful guides during my working life.

John Warren was my mentor for seven years at Shawmut Bank and Sterling Bank. He taught me the most valuable lesson of my working career – always do what's right. Like any good mentor, he never came right out and said it. He simply taught by example.

More recently, I have been blessed by a team of guides. Through my association with the BAM Alliance, a national community of independent advisors, I participate in a study group with 20 other advisory firms. Six of us have formed a peer group to further our development and learning. Scott Brown, Jeff Chernitzer, Steve Harvey, Bill Morgan, Al Sears and I have shared a group telephone call every other Friday morning for the past six years. We have been religious about not missing calls.

We share ideas on how to run our businesses, technical client issues, parents, children, marriage – no topic is off limits. These guys are great guides and teachers because they teach from love.

They all care more about the other group members than they do about themselves. These gentlemen have had a profound impact on my personal and professional development. They have helped me deal with adversity, learn from mistakes, and better understand my strengths and weaknesses as a practitioner and as a human being. They've been the guides I've needed in business and life.

Money and love

The days in the NICU were filled with difficult, dark hours. It was during these times that I would find my brain spinning around some very tough questions.

More than once, I wondered what I would do if the boys did not make it home. It was a heart-wrenching conversation with myself. What path would I take, both personally and professionally? Would I continue in my current job? Is this a meaningful career?

As I thought about this, my thoughts kept coming back to the nurses, our guides. This helped me appreciate why I do what I do. I realized that in my own small way, I act as a guide.

I help people find their way in uncertain and unfamiliar territory. I translate, define and interpret. I help clients look at the future with realistic expectations. I help balance fact and emotion. Most important, I help clients use their financial resources to lead more productive lives and express their love.

People first

About 20 years ago, I had the opportunity to take what I knew were very good institutional money manager jobs, but I turned them down. I now understand why. Those jobs, while interesting and challenging, lacked soul. Trading $2 billion a day was not very different or more meaningful than trading $2 a day. It just had more zeroes.

As a wealth advisor, I've found a priceless alignment between who I am and what I do.

> I know I'm doing something that makes a difference
> not just on a balance sheet or earnings report but in
> the lives of kind, interesting, hardworking people.

When I meet prospective clients for the first time, it's very common for them to express uncertainty, anxiety or even embarrassment about their investments and financial planning. Most new clients don't know much about investing, or retirement planning, or insurance and they don't really want to.

What they are looking for is a guide, someone to help them to use their hard-earned money to retire with dignity, or send a child to school, or give back to their community.

These are all acts of love.

My ideal job

Everyone has a story. My job is to listen to my clients' stories and help them write the next chapters. It is the perfect job for me. It's my gift. It fills me with satisfaction. It makes me tick.

Wondering if the boys would live, leaning on the support of the NICU nurses, and receiving countless calls and texts from caring people across the country taught me there is a lot more to life than numbers. It taught me nothing important in life is achieved on our own. Not success, not happiness, not peace of mind.

"In a dark place we find ourselves, and a little more knowledge lights our way." – Yoda

DISCUSS WITH YOUR ADVISOR

Who are the important guides in your life, and what have they taught you?

WHY JOHNNY CAN'T SAVE
2005

When the opportunity arose to teach a business class at Syracuse University, I jumped at it.

I taught an introductory course in entrepreneurship, a hot topic in the wake of the dot-com frenzy and eventual bubble. It was a great opportunity for me to help inspire the next wave of entrepreneurs and pass on the many lessons – both successes and disasters – I had learned in my own startup experience.

I felt it was a pretty good class, one I would have enjoyed when I was in college. But upon reflection, I'm not sure it was the class most of the students needed.

Most college kids graduate with significant debt and minimal understanding of saving, budgeting, borrowing or investing. Those fortunate enough to land a job with a decent salary are pretty much on their own to figure out how to manage their money and stay afloat financially.

Yes, there's some value to learning by trial and error, but some of the errors – such as choosing an apartment or car you can't afford, or running up big credit card bills – can be very costly. Bad money habits not only can land a young worker back in the parental home, they also can damage his or her credit rating for years.

For reasons I can't understand, the educational system has been slow to fill the financial literacy gap. Even a one-semester overview course on personal finance would help graduates get off on the right foot.

22

Financial Literacy Starts at Home

Every family's money situation is different. But wealthy or not, kids need some financial basics as they grow up and get ready to go out on their own.

The Programme for International Student Assessment recently completed an international financial literacy assessment of 15-year-olds. They did not do very well. Only 12 percent scored at the highest level of financial literacy and 22 percent scored below a baseline proficiency. U.S. teenagers scored in the middle of the pack.

I think the most interesting finding was that the performance on the financial literacy test had little to no relationship to the teenagers' math and reading skills. Even the kids that were "book smart" lacked the kind of basic knowledge and insight they would need to make good financial decisions.

Here are a few things you can do with your children or grandchildren to start them on the right track.

Spend, Save and Give

This simple, clever way to teach basic financial skills can begin at an early age. Get three glass jars and label them "Spend," "Save" and "Give." When your little one gets some birthday or holiday money, have him or her split the money between the three jars.

This is a great way to get a conversation started about the value of money and the different roles it can play.

One lesson is to watch how the jars change as money is added (or spent). You might be surprised how perceptive kids are about what it means when a jar is filling up or running low.

Another lesson is to give permission to spend on something inexpensive like candy or a small toy and then talk about saving for something a bit more lavish. Keep it within reason so they don't lose interest waiting.

The "Give" jar is full of potential conversations. Let your kids decide to whom they want to give. I bet they will surprise you.

The first bank account

You will eventually exhaust the learning possibilities of the jars. That marks a good time to graduate to a first bank account.

Assuming your child is still a minor, you will have to set up the account as a custodial account. This is easy to do and gives you joint access and control.

Let your son or daughter do as much of the paperwork as possible. It might take 10 minutes to fill out a deposit slip, but I guarantee you'll see a beaming face when that first deposit is made.

Go over the statements with them and continue to talk about spending, saving and giving. For my children, we always said saved money was "money for college." It seemed just exotic enough to keep their interest. When there was any inclination to give, I always matched the gift.

There may not be much interest earned, but do not miss the opportunity to point it out and discuss what it means. Remember that beyond the benefit of interest earned, putting money in the bank protects it from careless or needless spending. That is an important lifelong lesson.

Debit and credit cards

Most young adults have a difficult time understanding the difference between a debit card and a credit card. For most of us it is second nature, but ask your children. Really listen to their answers to hear if they understand the difference.

Walk them through a transaction on each type of account. They need to understand that a debit card directly accesses their bank account, while an unpaid credit card purchase is a loan from a finance company.

Help them understand that the downside to both cards is they make spending – and overspending – very easy. Lots of studies show that when no physical money leaves your pocket, it feels less like spending. Lots of little purchases add up quickly if you don't pay attention. With a debit card, this can be deadly, as your only spending limit is how much money you have in your account.

If you spend too much on a credit card, you'll end up paying interest, which is, in essence, a tax on lack of discipline.

Talk to your children about credit cards early and often, because the credit card companies will be after them as soon as they turn 18. (The walls of every college student union are plastered with credit card offers.)

Most young adults have a difficult time understanding what debt is and how interest payments work. Help them realize that credit card companies *want* them to maintain an unpaid balance and that minimum payments go mostly to interest, not principal. The numbers are chilling – a $1,000 balance with a 17 percent interest rate and a 1 percent minimum payment takes 205 months to pay off.

The flip side to all this is the real need for most adults to have a credit card. And it's not just about establishing credit to purchase a first home. Many insurance companies and landlords run credit checks as part of the application process. Even some employers check credit history to gauge a candidate's level of responsibility. Without a credit card, there may be no credit history to check. This is especially important if you are paying your child's cell phone, utility, rent and cable bills.

If your child does open a credit card account, be sure the initial credit limit is set very low. And for both credit and debit cards, review with your child how to check balances online. The only way to keep spending in check is to watch it on a regular basis.

529 Plans

Kids need to understand that going to college is a huge financial commitment for the whole family. Putting away money throughout their early years will reduce the burden when they head off to school. Children can save only so much, so you, as a parent or grandparent, will need to do most of the saving and investing.

Consider setting up a 529 plan, a savings and investing plan specifically for educational expenses. A 529 plan is operated by a state and can be used to meet the costs of qualified colleges nationwide. The plans work like an Individual Retirement Account (IRA), with investments in stocks and bonds and tax-free growth.

This is a great way for grandparents to make a difference for their grandkids. I have seen the real-world effects of my father opening

529 plan accounts for my older children, Austin and Charlotte. It was nice to hear them talking about the contributions and how the account had grown, or not, due to changes in the market. It also reiterated the importance that our family places on higher education, with the message coming from Grampy and not solely from Mom or Dad.

The accounts are easy to open via the Internet and are self-service. There's no need to pay someone to assist you.

Protect your private information

According to the University of Texas, children are up to 35 times more likely than adults to have their identities stolen. The most misused piece of information is the Social Security number. Teach your child to think twice before giving out this valuable piece of data. It is okay to ask why it is needed and how it will be protected. Chances are the local soccer league does not really need your child's Social Security number.

Go online and show your kids examples of phishing websites. When you know to look at website addresses (URLs), it becomes much easier to determine what is fake and what is not. If you get an email from a fraudster, show it to them. Have them read it and help them spot the bad grammar and ridiculous need to "send money urgently."

When they venture out of the house, make sure your kids understand the dangers of using unsecured networks. It may be fun to buy a book from Amazon while enjoying a coffee at Starbucks, but that online transaction can be risky if the network is not secure.

Roth IRAs

It's unlikely that your child knows much about Roth IRAs, but summer jobs mean paychecks, and anyone with earned income can contribute to a Roth IRA. It will not be easy to get them to contribute their own money, so consider making the first few contributions yourself to get things started. You might get them interested if you match some or all of their contributions.

Your kids certainly will not care about retirement income, so instead focus on the effect of compounding. The math is pretty neat given how many years they have for the investment to grow. A $1,000 investment grows to almost $47,000 in 50 years at an 8 percent return. I bet they will think $47,000 is a lot of money for doing nothing but being patient.

In a Roth IRA, I would suggest a passively managed, diversified stock mutual fund that is low in costs and fees.

Talking about a Roth with your children is a great starter conversation that can bridge over to participation in their company 401(k) plan when they join the full-time workforce.

Wants versus needs

One of the hardest lessons to learn as an independent young adult revolves around wants versus needs. Most young people have basically spent their entire life with all their needs paid for. They had to fund only their wants. A lot of young adults get into financial trouble because they continue to put their wants first (the newest cell phone, a luxury car on a lease, an expensive vacation).

Early in one's career it's just not financially feasible to have all your wants. Needs must come first, and it may take many months or years to save up for wants. Regardless of age, it really comes down to the lessons of the "Spend," "Save" and "Give" jars. Be prepared to reinforce this idea with your kids.

Stay involved as your kids go out on their own. Don't count on the educational system, employers or friends to teach your kids about money. Lessons about overspending are especially critical. If your children can't afford to fund their company 401(k) plan, it is a spending issue, not an earning issue. If their credit card balances continue to grow, it is a spending issue.

If there's one big theme in all of these ideas, it's to get the conversation about money started at an early age and keep it going. Be honest about your own experiences, both positive and negative. If you wait for your kids to make big money mistakes before you start the conversation, the consequences can be expensive.

DISCUSS WITH YOUR ADVISOR

What is the best lesson you learned about money
when you were young?

STARTING OVER
2011

Sometimes things don't go as you expect.

When my first wife and I celebrated our marriage on a beautiful autumn day in 1992, I looked forward to a small family, a successful career and a nice home. The standard ingredients of a good marriage and happy life.

While there were many priceless rewards in the marriage, ultimately the partnership did not last. Outside of our mutual and infinite love for Austin and Charlotte, we eventually found ourselves not only on different pages but reading from very different books.

These were difficult days. Where there had once been companionship, love and warmth I found rejection and confusion. Thankfully, the kids, in their innocent wisdom, helped us both get through the worst of it, without taking sides.

In retrospect, I know divorce was the right decision for us. Nonetheless, it was hard. We were throwing the kids into a whole new world, and I found myself starting over at age 50, financially and emotionally.

I moved into a barely furnished rented house, collecting hand-me-down furniture and housewares from friends. It was back to living paycheck to paycheck like a new college grad. The marriage was over. The dream was over. It seemed obvious: Nothing good could ever happen again. Not being able to tuck my kids in every night was unbearable.

On top of the emotional strain I felt, I must be honest: My financial picture was a mess.

23

Life after Divorce

Divorce is not just about splitting up. It's also about pulling things together afterward. Almost half of married couples in the U.S. go through this process, but that doesn't make it any easier.

I imagine you will read this chapter only if you are somewhere in the divorce process or think you might be sometime in the future. With that in mind, I offer you my understanding and encouragement. Even if it seems overwhelming right now, you will get through it. Dark days will eventually brighten.

For now, I'll share some thoughts that may be helpful to you, with the giant disclaimer that every divorce is unique. Yours may be friendly or mean, fast or drawn out. Get legal guidance to help you sort out the options and constraints that apply in your specific situation.

We used a mediator to help draft our divorce agreement and found it to be an acceptable solution. But you may require attorneys on both sides from the start, especially if child custody or other key items are in dispute.

Divide

Fairly early in the process you will need to compile a complete inventory of assets. That includes all savings, investment and retirement accounts, as well as real estate, business interests, cars, boats, country club memberships, antiques, artwork and other items of value.

Your divorce agreement and prevailing state law will determine how these assets are divided between you and your spouse.

Not all assets are subject to division, but put everything on the list to be sure. For instance, money you personally inherited and have kept in a separate account in your name may be excluded from marital assets and the division process. Consult your attorney or mediator on items like these.

You will also need to agree on how liabilities and responsibilities will be divided or shared after the divorce.

- Where will the kids spend their time, and who will pay for their care?
- Who will pay for college?
- Who will stay in and pay the mortgage on the family home?
- Who will be responsible for outstanding car or college loans?
- If you own a business together, will you continue to work together?

Assess

As it becomes clear how assets and responsibilities will be distributed, it's time to take a deep breath and assess where you are financially.

This assessment can cover many elements of financial health, but let's start with the most basic gauge – cash flow. Cash flow is the fancy term for money-in and money-out.

What will your financial responsibilities be every
month, and how will you pay for them?

This is Budgeting 101, of course. Make a list of monthly bills –
housing, utilities, car loan, food, insurance, healthcare, clothing,
phone, Internet and all of the other expenses as they will be in
your new reality. Then add all the other things you expect to
spend money on – entertainment, travel, gifts, hobbies.

Then add allotments for things you hope you won't pay for but
probably will – car repairs, home repairs and other surprises.
Finally, add a line item for retirement savings – a consistent
contribution every month, deducted automatically from your
checking account.

Compare the total of all these outlays to the money-in side of the
ledger. Is your monthly after-tax income sufficient to consistently
cover all the expenses?

If not, something has to give. Because if nothing changes, the
shortfall will accumulate on your credit cards, putting you much
further behind over time.

Many people find they can close a modest shortfall by cutting
back on discretionary expenses like dining out. But if the shortfall
is too large to fix with small sacrifices, you'll need to look at the
bigger-ticket items. That may mean downsizing to a smaller home
or apartment, moving to a less expensive community, or scaling
back on how and how often you travel.

Many of these changes will seem unappetizing, but all options
must be on the table. It's impossible to eliminate a persistent
monthly shortfall without fundamentally changing the money-
in/money-out equation.

Adjust

Depending on your situation, there may be other financial and legal matters to attend to post-divorce.

For starters, key documents like your will, living will, power of attorney and healthcare proxy may need updating to reflect the new shape of your family.

Likewise, if your spouse is listed as beneficiary on any insurance policy or retirement account, you may want to change the beneficiary to your children or other loved ones.

You may also find your need for life insurance is greater or less than it was when you were married. If your children are grown and in good financial shape, for instance, there may be no clear need for keeping your policy.

Finally, take a fresh look at your plans for retirement, meaning both how you want to live and how you will pay for it.

Your retirement scenario may have changed considerably. You may find you have significantly less (or more) in your retirement accounts. Talk to your investment advisor about how much to add to your account each month to finance the kind of retirement you foresee. You may find you'll need to work longer than you previously thought.

Breathe

Even "easy" divorces are hard. And the changes that come afterward can be challenging too. However, for many couples and their children, it is the best path forward. If you find yourself on this path, hang in there and be sure to reach out to friends and professionals to help you through it.

DISCUSS WITH YOUR ADVISOR

If you are facing a divorce, do you have a financial plan that protects you and your loved ones?

TIME TO PLANT SOME TREES
2017

While we had two boys in the NICU, Lori and I bought a new house AND moved. Yes, it was crazy, but it was also necessary. We needed more room. We needed a house that was ours, not mine.

We are blessed. It is a beautiful home in a wonderful neighborhood. It has enough room for our new, enlarged Brady Bunch family.

But what I am most excited about is the back yard.

I spent many hours rocking sick little boys, daydreaming about two healthy boys running around our new back yard. It is almost an acre, all grass, a blank canvas for fun and games. And a little horticulture.

My maternal grandfather was a dairy farmer and an extraordinary vegetable gardener. I know there is a bit of farmer in my soul. Whenever I've had any extra yard space, I've planted a vegetable garden.

Our new yard will most certainly have a vegetable garden. I have already picked out the spot.

I'm also going to try something new. I'll soon be planting a few fruit trees. I think the fruit trees will be a wonderful project for Nathan, Charlie and me.

We will all benefit from the fresh air and exercise as we plant and tend to the trees. Not to mention the pleasure of eating fresh fruit straight from the source.

I think we might also learn some greater life lessons along the way.

24

Less Is More

I'm a doer. When our fruit trees go into the ground, I will be anxious to take action, early and often, to coax them to optimal health. My instinct will be to overwater, add too much fertilizer and peek at the roots. I must resist this instinct.

Our fruit trees won't look like much in the beginning. They'll look half sick for a couple of years. It will be hard for me to calmly wait and let nature work. Patience is not my natural mode of operation.

Nonetheless, patience is what the trees need from me. I need to follow the directions and stay on plan. I need to keep it simple. When I do not know what to do, I should probably do nothing.

With plants and trees, matters are seldom made worse by doing nothing and are often made much worse by frequent and inept intervention.

The same can be said for investing.

Although it seems smart and responsible to carefully tend our investments, it is very easy – and perilous – to overdo it. The more we pay attention to our long-term investments and, for lack of a better word, fiddle with them, the more likely we are to hurt, not help, our results.

Stay the course

Sound investment strategy, like growing good fruit trees, requires a measure of discipline and dose of detachment. Investing rewards persistence and consistency, and exacts penalties for needless tinkering.

I will have to water the newly planted trees on a very consistent schedule, not just when it is convenient. The boys will most certainly find this portion of the project boring, but if we stick with it, the trees should grow and ultimately bear fruit.

Persistence and consistency are both simple but not easy. The physical process of watering trees is certainly simple. The tricky parts are finding the time, not forgetting, not being lazy and sticking to it even when the payoff seems so far in the future.

Sounds like investing to me. Don't we all wish we could speak to our twenty-something selves about the simple but not easy task of adding money to a retirement plan on every payday? All we had to do was put our long-term welfare ahead of short-term gratification, laziness and distraction. Just sticking to the simple plan was all we needed.

Persistence and consistency sound so mundane, but when combined, they can produce magical results. Water and ignore the trees, and eventually you get loads of fruit. If you have ever grown anything, you probably know how even a small harvest can feel a bit magical.

In investing, the magic of patience is expressed through the power of compound interest. Like watering trees, compound interest is boring. There's no immediate gratification. Most of the time, it seems like it's not doing anything at all, but then magically its impact emerges.

How magically? Consider this example. Invest $5,000 a year in a 401(k) plan. For discussion, let's use an 8 percent annual rate of return.

After 10 years, you have a little more than $72,000 (not that big a deal, as you have put in $50,000).

After 25 years, your account grows to about $365,000 (versus your $125,000 investment, this is pretty good but still not a fortune).

After 45 years and contributions of $225,000, your account surpasses $1.9 million! Like magic.

Expect bad weather

Growing fruit trees in Central New York guarantees me only one thing: There will be bad weather.

It is a certainty the trees will face long periods of very low temperatures. The trees will look terrible without their leaves half of every year. The snow will pile halfway up the trunks. On many days, I will wonder if they are even alive.

Investors inevitably face bad weather as well. It doesn't follow a calendar like the weather, but sooner or later the stock market is sure to turn gloomy, cold and dark. Amid bad economic or political news, stock values can fall like autumn foliage, leaving investors feeling like growth and prosperity will never return.

It would be easy to think I should dig
the trees up every winter and bring them into the
garage to protect them. But that is the worst
choice I could make.

What I need to do is leave them alone, stay calm and remember they are not dead but dormant. They are dormant because nature knows winter is coming. The trees protect their long-term prospects by storing energy until spring.

Staying relaxed and disciplined during down stock markets is hard. When prices fall, it can be tempting to sell everything and seek refuge in the garage. But this is no more productive than pulling trees out of the ground every winter. To make money in the stock market, you need to stay invested.

Stormy markets are unpleasant, but in hindsight, we can see these downturns are as temporary as winter. What looks and feels dead is only dormant.

Plant more than one tree

I plan to plant several trees and a few different varieties. I would be amazed if they all survived and produced fruit. I'm sure I will have to plant more trees in the future.

This is par for the course in horticulture. The various trees will probably have differing tolerances for soil conditions and weather. Some may have bountiful years when others are limping along. But if I have multiple trees, I should never be without any fruit.

A diversified stock portfolio is much the same. It should hold thousands of companies across multiple industries and countries. In any given year, some companies will do well. Others will struggle. Even if some companies fail at some point, the portfolio as a whole will live on.

Leave a legacy

The back corner of our yard is a nice spot for the new fruit trees. It is sunny and has good soil. The boys and I will water them regularly, prune occasionally, and leave them alone and let them grow.

If we do our part, these trees should bear fruit long after I am gone. My children should enjoy the result of this labor, and with any luck, my children's children will too. With a little thoughtful care and a lot of patience, we're creating something for the future.

By the same token, if you are a good saver and patient investor, control your spending, and stick to a long-term plan, your investments should outlive you and be there for your children and your children's children.

DISCUSS WITH YOUR ADVISOR

Are you approaching your investments
with patience and discipline?

I OWN A WRENCH, BUT I'M NO PLUMBER
2015

When I was buying my small home after getting divorced, I knew it needed lots of work.

Walking through the place, I made two mental lists.

The first list was "Do it myself." I knew I could handle painting and minor carpentry. I figured I could patch the foundation where some mortar had cracked and crumbled. I was up for the challenge of rebuilding the porch.

The second list, "Hire a professional," had plenty of items too. I definitely needed help with plumbing work. I'd need some help with the kitchen and bath upgrades. Refinishing the floors and stairs required tools, skills and patience I knew I didn't have.

We make these decisions all the time – do it yourself or let someone with more knowledge, experience and specialized tools take care of it in half the time.

Sometimes we make the wrong decision. I replaced the lights in my kitchen on my own. I got the wiring right and the lights worked fine. But I put them in the wrong places, so I had to open the ceiling up again to move them. Whatever I had saved by doing it myself I paid for in rework and frustration.

25

Finding the Right Advisor

Investing was never a do-it-yourself possibility until the 1990s, when companies like eTrade and Ameritrade provided anyone with a personal computer a dial-up door to the stock market. Now you can invest on your phone when you're stuck in traffic. But should you?

Of course, it is your decision whether you work with a wealth manager or go it alone.

To be honest, if I weren't in the investment field, I would probably try to manage my own financial plan and portfolio. From the outside, it doesn't look difficult, and I would wonder if an advisor really adds enough value to make it worthwhile.

But having worked with hundreds of people who have done it themselves, I can say with complete conviction that a professional advisor makes a huge difference.

Here are five areas where do-it-yourself investors often get it wrong when managing their own finances:

1. Lack of diversification
2. High fees and expenses
3. Inappropriate asset allocation
4. Lack of rebalancing
5. Tax inefficiencies

A wealth advisor (who may also be called a *wealth manager, financial planner* or *investment advisor*) can easily spot do-it-yourself inefficiencies like these and fix them, just like an experienced mechanic can quickly diagnose and repair a sputtering engine.

In most situations, an advisor can make portfolio improvements that far exceed his or her fee, not to mention help the client put in place trusts and estate plans to protect loved ones and reduce taxes.

If you are looking for an advisor, the following thoughts may help you find one who's right for you. Here are four questions to ask any prospective advisor:

Are you a fiduciary?

The fiduciary standard is a legal requirement to work in the best interests of clients in every situation. This seems like an obvious requirement, but many so-called advisors are not required to act as a fiduciary; they are free to put their own interests first.

It turns out many financial professionals are really salespeople, paid specifically to sell certain families of mutual funds, annuities or other products. These non-fiduciary representatives may pick products for you based on the size of their commission, not on how well the products will meet your needs. That's the definition of *conflict of interest*, and for many advisors, including most stockbrokers, it's perfectly legal.

All professionals designated as registered investment advisors (RIAs) are fiduciaries. If an advisor is not an RIA, be sure to ask if he or she is a fiduciary.

How do you get paid?

This is another way to verify that you are talking to a fiduciary. A fiduciary works for you and is paid by you, usually through a quarterly or annual fee based on the size of your portfolio. A fiduciary never receives commissions or other compensation from mutual fund companies or other product providers.

> If an advisor is receiving compensation from other entities, the advice provided cannot be considered independent and unbiased.

How will you choose investments for me?

As I have discussed throughout this book, there is no reason to expect that any advisor can systematically and consistently predict future market movements. Therefore, any advisor who describes a sophisticated model or system for identifying parts of the market that will outperform (*active management*) should be treated with skeptical caution. Remember, no one knows in advance which stocks will do best or when to get in or out of the market.

Look for an advisor who focuses on choosing an asset allocation that is appropriate for your situation and goals, not on prediction. This kind of advisor will recommend mutual funds with hundreds or thousands of securities in each asset class, seeking to replicate – not exceed – the performance of each class (*passive management*). He or she will not make any claim about beating the market or knowing which segments of the market will perform better or worse than average.

Some advisors may try to avoid the word *passive*, as it can have a negative connotation in other contexts, but in investing it should not be considered a dirty word. In essence, a passive approach is one that accepts the generosity of capitalism, without wasting time and energy on predictive techniques that cannot be relied upon.

Who are you?

The first three questions are about investing. This last one is about the advisor as a person. If you pick the right advisor, you will likely be working with him or her for decades, so personal connection and trust are important.

As you consider your options for a wealth advisor, this checklist of what to look for – and what to avoid – may be helpful:

What to look for	What to avoid
Long-term focus and perspective	Market timing and stock picking
Emphasis on YOUR long-term goals, hopes and dreams	Emphasis on beating the market
Behavioral coaching	Speculation and performance chasing
A personalized Investment Policy Statement	Market and economic forecasting
Discipline	Analysis of current events to uncover trading opportunities

Look for a person who is interested in you and your family, someone who communicates well, and someone with whom you feel comfortable sharing the details of your life, goals and career, both good and bad.

DISCUSS WITH YOUR ADVISOR

Do you favor active or passive investment management?

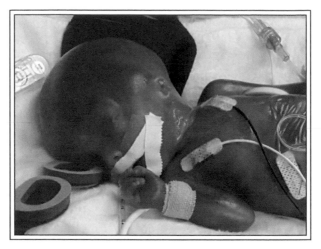

Nathan – One day old.

Charlie – 24 days old. Lori finally gets to hold one of her babies.

Epilogue

Nathan came home from the NICU on Day 100, July 12, 2016. We had to wait 58 more days for Charlie to come home on September 8.

Lori and I were scared, nervous, tired and hopeful. The boys were growing, but they needed to be fed every three hours, and they both had ostomy bags to deal with following their surgeries for perforated intestines.

It was a giant relief to have everyone under one roof, but we knew normalcy was a long way off.

We spent the winter worrying about sickness and infection. Because their health had many times turned on a dime, getting them safely to their first birthday looked like a long uphill road.

Winter brought new worries, as upstate New York was hit with a very potent stomach bug strain. It made our ears ring with the parting words from our NICU team: "Just get those two boys through their first winter." We doubled down on cleaning the house and keeping people away. Only people necessary for the boys' care were allowed in.

January arrived, and our worst nightmare was realized when Nathan contracted the stomach bug and landed in the hospital with dehydration. It was downhill from there. Within two days, Charlie, Lori and I caught the same virus, and all four of us had to check into the hospital.

Charlie got well in a few days, but Nathan needed a couple more days in the hospital to get stronger. The extended stay gave him enough time to be exposed to another nightmare – bacteria. He became so sick, he almost did not make it. Lori and I were hanging on by a very thin thread as the infectious disease team tried to isolate the germ.

After spending all that time in the NICU with the boys being so close to death for all those days, it was indescribably hard to be back to this again. Back to worrying our way through agonizing unknowns.

Two and a half days later, the infectious disease team was able to isolate the bacteria as something called *gram-negative rods*. If it sounds bad, that's because it is. The good news was it was treatable. Another disaster dodged.

We spent the rest of January and February praying the boys would stay healthy and grow a little in preparation for the next big hurdle – intestinal reconnection surgery.

The reconnection surgeries were relatively easy, but the recovery was very difficult. All four of us slept in the hospital as we waited for their digestive systems to fully work for the first time.

Fourteen maddening days later, two little boys pooped. There was much rejoicing! I can't express how draining and difficult that final hurdle was and how sweet it was to finally go home for good.

Eleven months after the twins were born, it finally seemed like it was time to just start living.

As I write this, the boys are 15 months old. Nathan is over 18 pounds and Charlie has broken 19 pounds. I get tears in my eyes every time they do something new.

Epilogue

I have never taken a single day for granted as a father, but raising Austin and Charlotte was a completely different experience. Not better or worse, just different.

With Nathan and Charlie, reaching 15 months seems like a miracle. Their crying is sweet music because I will never forget when they were too sick to cry. Sitting up and rolling over are bringing cheers.

We continue to be blessed with incredible medical professionals. People who seemingly care as much about our children as we do. When we have graduated from one care provider to another, there are always hugs and tears of deep, deep appreciation.

Summer is here, the windows are open and we now welcome visitors with open arms. If you ever want to see what a miracle looks like, please stop by. I can show you two of them.

Charlie – 15 months old

Nathan – 15 months old

Thank you

To Austin and Charlotte. It has been pure joy watching you grow. From beautiful babies to interesting adults, you have made me proud every single day. Thank you for welcoming your new baby brothers with open arms. There will always be room for all of us. Go out there and change the world for the better. You both can do it. I love you more than you know.

To Areya for coming into my life and for accepting me into your life. I love having you be part of our expanding family. You too can change the world.

To Mom and Dad for all you have done and continue to do. Thank you for allowing me to be me. I know that is not easy for a parent. Thank you for all the support you have provided me; it is the greatest gift anyone has given me. I am so happy that you got to meet Nathan and Charlie. It has been one of my greatest pleasures.

I am grateful for my brother, Michael. You have always been there, supporting me and encouraging me. It is greatly appreciated.

To Grampa Ray and Grandma Barb Lichorobiec. Thank you for everything you do. We could not have made it through this past year without you.

I am grateful for the entire BAM Alliance community, with special thanks to the BAM Masters Forum. You are friends and mentors. I would not be who I am professionally without your constant encouragement. To Meredith Boggess for encouraging me to write this book. Finally, to Al, Jeff, Steve, Bill and Scott – you are like brothers.

To John O'Leary for encouraging me – and everyone else – to tell their story. Please don't stop doing what you do.

To my partners and colleagues at FMF&E Wealth Management and Firley, Moran, Freer & Eassa, CPA. Thank you for providing me with a platform to do my life's work. Special thanks to April Mueller for your daily commitment to do the right thing.

This book would not exist without my lifelong friend Steve Mott. You have a way with words. You are a great friend and an even better person. Thanks, pal.

To all the people that propped us up this past year. The people of Skaneateles proved what friendship means day after day. We were continually amazed at the outpouring of love. Special thanks to Mike, Dave and Rick. Your constant emails, texts and phone calls helped keep me together.

To all the people, known and unknown, who took time out their lives this past year to pray for Nathan and Charlie. There are hundreds of you from coast to coast. I can never repay your kindness. Thank you from the bottom of my heart.

In the fall of 1978, I arrived on the campus of St. Bonaventure University, and some part of me has never left. Thirty-nine years later, the ties that bind have only grown tighter. We have celebrated countless joys and endured a few sorrows. Through thick and thin, the Bonas family has been there. To Joe, Garrie, Pat, SuSu and Krups for stepping into the godparent role. You are the perfect choice. To Fr. Frank for performing a wonderful Baptism.

To the many doctors and nurses that took care of our children as if they were their own. Special thanks to the miracle workers at the Crouse Hospital NICU, the Center for Children's Surgery at Upstate and the Center for Pediatric Gastroenterology at Upstate.

To our "little fighters" – Nathan and Charlie. I have witnessed a miracle only because you both wanted so much to be here. You are strong of will and heart. You have taught me that every day has meaning. I can't wait to watch you grow up. You are going to be something special. ("The more difficulties one has to encounter, within and without, the more significant and the higher in inspiration his life will be." – Horace Bushnell) I love you both.

My deepest gratitude is for Lori, my beautiful wife and the love of my life. Your strength and devotion have been an inspiration. You taught me how to be an advocate for our children, how to stay strong in the darkest hours and what true faith means. You should never forget what they said about you in the NICU: "These boys picked you as their mother because they knew you would never give up on them." Truer words have never been spoken. I truly believe that there is one person who can completely turn your world around. You are that person. I love you.

SOURCES AND DESCRIPTIONS OF DATA

S&P 500 Index. The S&P Data are provided by Standard & Poor's Index Services Group.

Large Companies. S&P 500 Index. The S&P Data are provided by Standard & Poor's Index Services Group.

Small Companies. Dimensional US Small Cap Index. Dimensional Index data compiled by Dimensional.

One-Month U.S. Treasury Bills. One-Month US Treasury Bills. Source: Morningstar. Former Source: *Stocks, Bonds, Bills and Inflation*, Ibbotson and Sinquefield, 1986.

Long-Term U.S. Government Bonds. Long Term Government Bonds. Source: Morningstar. Former Source: Stock, Bonds, Bills and Inflation, Ibbotson and Sinquefield, 1986.

Inflation. U.S. Consumer Price Index. Represented by Consumer Price Index for All Urban Consumer (CPI–U), not seasonally adjusted. Source: US long-term bonds, bills, inflation, and fixed income factor data ©*Stocks, Bonds, Bills, and Inflation Yearbook*™, Ibbotson Associates, Chicago (annually updated work by Roger G. Ibbotson and Rex A. Sinquefield).

Do Stocks Outperform Treasury Bills? Hendrik Bessembinder, Department of Finance, W.P. Carey School of Business, Arizona State University. Draft dated May 2017.

ABOUT THE AUTHOR

Chris Gardner is president of FMF&E Wealth Management, LLC, in Syracuse, New York. As a wealth advisor, Chris helps people find peace of mind about their finances so they can live the life they love.

Chris holds an MBA from Northeastern University and a BBA from St. Bonaventure University. He is passionate about the Syracuse Rescue Mission and has served on its board of directors for several years.

Chris lives in Skaneateles, New York, with his wife, Lori, and their children. He loves to read, play golf, go boating, and build and grow things, but he mostly chases around his twin sons. He is blessed.

Chris can be reached via email at cgardner@fmfewealthmgt.com.

For more information

For more information about this book, additional photos and family updates, please visit personalfinancestory.com.